The Great Edwardian Gardens of Harold Peto

The Great Edwardian

Gardens of Harold Peto

FROM THE ARCHIVES OF COUNTRY LIFE

ROBIN WHALLEY

AURUM PRESS

First published in Great Britain 2007 by Aurum Press Limited
25 Bedford Avenue, London WC1B 3AT
www.aurumpress.co.uk

ISBN 978 1 84513 235 4
10 9 8 7 6 5 4 3 2 1
2011 2010 2009 2008 2007

Design by James Campus
Originated, printed and bound in Singapore by CS Graphics

Frontispiece: Easton Lodge, Essex.
Front endpaper: Iford Manor, Wiltshire.
Rear endpaper: Villa Sylvia, Alpes-Maritimes.

THE COUNTRY LIFE PICTURE LIBRARY

The *Country Life* Picture Library holds a complete set of prints made from its negatives,
and a card index to the subjects, usually recording the name of the photographer and the date
of the photographs catalogued, together with a separate index of photographers.
It also holds a complete set of *Country Life* and various forms of published indices to the
magazine. The Library may be visited by appointment, and prints of any negatives it holds
can be supplied by post.

For further information, please contact the Librarian, Camilla Costello, at *Country Life*,
King's Reach Tower, Stamford Street, London SE1 9LS (*Tel*: 020 7261 6337).

ACKNOWLEDGEMENTS

Many archivists and librarians have been very generous with their help; I would particularly
like to thank John d'Arcy and the staff at the Wiltshire Record Office and Sharon-Michi
Kusunoki, Archivist at West Dean College. I am very grateful to Joachim Wolschke-Bulmahn,
Linda Lott and the other staff at Dumbarton Oaks for their support during my fellowship
there; and to the other fellows, who helped to make my stay in Washington stimulating and
enjoyable. During the time I have been writing on Harold Peto, I have made many friends
and contacts, who have been very forthcoming with their time and knowledge and I am most
grateful to the following: Ian Alderman, Jane Avner, Jane Balfour, Rita Boswell, Graham
Davies, Simon Dorrell, Nigel Everett, Lord Faringdon, Tom Faulkner, Cormac Foley, Robin
and Wendy Goffe, Hilary Grainger, Maryann Harris, May Brawley Hill, Colin Hiscock, Simon
Hoare, Penelope Hobhouse, Erica Hunningher, Mary Keen, Tony Lowes, Marion Mako,
Caroline Mathieu, Anne and Arthur Mead, Sir George Meyrick, Michael Mitchell, Graeme
Moore, Tim Mowl, Orla Murphy, Peter Newall, the late Michael Newcombe, the late Bernard
Pardoe, Maureen Pearce, Guy Rasch and his parents, Wendy Reynolds, David and Elizabeth
Salkeld, Tim Schroder, Susan Sinclair, Judith Tankard, Geoffrey Theed, Jeffrey Thomas,
Richard Tomlinson, Michael Tooley, Alison and Martin Trowell, Nigel Tudor-Craig, Arpad
Turmezei, Ann Uppington, Sybil Wade, William Waterfield, David Welch, David Wheeler,
and my former colleagues and the library staff at Bath Spa University.

I am indebted to the owners for access to Peto's gardens and for sharing with me their
knowledge of his commissions. The commitment to restoring these outstanding gardens has
been unstinting, and in this respect I would especially like to acknowledge Brian and Diana
Creasey, who have made so much material available to me, and given enormously of their
time and resources to initiate the restoration of the gardens of Easton Lodge. Also, the owners
of Iford Manor, Elizabeth and John Hignett, who have nurtured its spirit and fabric over
many years, and have been so enthusiastic in assisting with my unending quest.

I owe a very special thanks to many members of the Peto family and their relatives, who
have contributed to my knowledge of Harold. In particular, I would like to thank Richard and
Jo Earle, who have indicated so many new lines of enquiry, Jonathan Peto for access to family
records and Sir Henry Peto for providing the portrait of Harold and his brothers. I have had
unequalled support from Harold's great niece, Lady Matheson and her daughter Nell, who
have helped in many unimaginable ways to give me a sense of Harold's character and draw
my attention to the wonderful diaries that he wrote, which are now deposited in the Wiltshire
Record Office.

It has been an inspiring time to bring this book to fruition for which I am extremely
grateful to Kathryn Bradley-Hole, the Gardens Editor of *Country Life*, to Camilla Costello and
the staff of the *Country Life* Picture Library, to Clare Howell, who has been such a perceptive
and encouraging editor to work with, and James Campus who has been at such pains to
incorporate my suggestions to make the text and photographs such a tribute to the great
gardens of Harold Peto.

However, I could not have brought this research together had it not been for the unfailing
support, as well as the scholarly and discerning advice, of my wife, Karin Hiscock.

LIST OF ARTICLES

The following is a list of *Country Life* articles from which the photographs in this book have
been reproduced. The photographer's name is given in brackets where known.

Alcazar, Seville, Spain: 7 January 1899.

Alhambra, Granada, Spain: 19 November 1898.

Bridge House, Surrey: 24 October 1908; 1 April 1916.

Burton Pynsent, Somerset: 6 October 1934 (A. E. Henson).

Buscot Park, Oxfordshire: 21 October 1916; 18 and 25 May 1940 (A. E. Henson); 1 July 2004
    (Clive Boursnell).

Crichel, Dorset: 18 January 1908; 16, 23 and 30 May 1925 (A. E. Henson).

Duncombe Park, North Yorkshire: 25 February 1905.

Easton Lodge, Essex: 23 November 1907; 1 May 1909; 25 September 2003.

Generalife, Granada, Spain: 1898; 16 December 1916.

Hartham Park, Wiltshire: 7 August 1909.

Heale House, Wiltshire: 27 February 1915; 29 November 1984 (Jonathan Gibson).

Heronden, Kent: 11 and 18 August 1960 (Alex Starkey).

High Wall, Oxfordshire: 10 and 17 November 1917.

Hinton Admiral, Hampshire: 8 October 1910.

Iford Manor, Wiltshire: 28 September 1907; 11 October 1913; 26 August and 2 September
    1922 (Sleigh); 4 April 1963; 18 May 1972 (Jonathan Gibson).

Ilnacullin (Garinish Island), Co. Cork, Ireland: 11 March 1965; *Colour illustrations*: 2006
    (Marianne Majerus).

Isola Bella, Cannes: 1 April 1911.

Japan, Gardens: 14 September and 16 November 1901; 22 February 1902; 8 October 1959.

Maryland, Alpes-Maritimes: 3 and 10 December 1910.

Montacute House, Somerset: 16 and 23 April 1898; 4 June 1904; 12 and 19 June 1915; 20 and
    27 October and 3 November 1955 (A. E. Henson).

Petwood, Lincolnshire: 7 August 1915.

Pitchford Hall, Shropshire: 2 February 1901; 7 and 14 April 1917.

St. Catherine's Court, Somerset: 24 December 1898; 24 November and 1 December 1906.

Somerleyton Hall, Suffolk: 3 June 1982 (C. Hall).

Treillage: *Notes on the Art of Treillage I & II*, 18 and 25 September 1909.

Villa Rosemary, Alpes-Maritimes: 30 March 1912; 14 January 1928.

Villa Salles, Alpes-Maritimes: 18 December 1926.

Villa Sylvia, Alpes-Maritimes: 16 July 1910; 15 January 1927.

Wayford Manor, Wiltshire: 29 September 1934 (A. E. Henson); 7 March 1985 (Alex Starkey).

West Dean, Sussex: 29 July 1899; 22 and 29 October 1981 (Jonathan Gibson); 2 March 1995
    (Clive Boursnell); *Colour illustrations*: 2006 (Marianne Majerus).

Westbury Court, Gloucestershire: 12 September 1903; 19 December 1908.

PICTURE CREDITS

CONTENTS

LOOKING BACK over the twentieth century, the Edwardian period has assumed the character of a belle époque. So much has been written about that time, which spans the years following the death of Queen Victoria in 1901 to the outbreak of the relentless, futile and dehumanising war in Europe. It is a gross irony that this halcyon interlude should have ended with such a catastrophic disaster. Although general historical and social studies of this piquant era have not entirely confirmed the tranquil picture associated with a summer of lazy afternoons, the record of garden-making at this juncture lends credence to an astonishingly creative period; a period which is still dominated by a vision of the garden with its quintessential country house surrounded by billowing yew hedges, architectural topiary, steps and terraces. It was this vision that for the most part disappeared following the end of the First World War, or was replaced by the Modernist garden of the 1920s and 1930s.

Many owners, designers and gardeners expressed this burgeoning of creativity, and yet from a general overview of these years it would appear that Gertrude Jekyll and Edwin Lutyens have so illuminated our visual memory that the many other brilliant exponents of garden art have been obscured. These two eminent Edwardians have justifiably received much attention, not least because they both compiled a surviving comprehensive record of their activities. In the case of many others though, like Inigo Thomas and Harold Peto, the gardens are isolated from documentation and have largely been left to speak for themselves, as much of the material about their making has been lost. However, both Peto and Thomas left behind gardens of the utmost ingenuity, colour and inspired architectural work that are their enduring legacy.

The work of Harold Peto, as illustrated in *Country Life*, is the trail by which we can find our way back and retrace our steps to that 'golden age'. The gardens provide significant moments that are the keys to unlocking some of the preoccupations of that time, a rapidly changing world of increased mobility, travel and tourism, a time when the Murray handbooks to foreign lands were published and updated year upon year, becoming the indispensable guide to accompany every traveller to Europe and beyond. Experiences of gardens and countries, including the Far East, were to fuel Peto with the energy that nurtured his imagination and with a poetic sensibility which manifested itself in memories of the past. For, as he said, 'Old buildings or fragments of Masonry carry one's mind back to the past in a way that a

garden entirely of flowers cannot do'. This sensitivity to history brings unique qualities to his work and distinguishes it from that of his contemporaries.

Peto's Compeers

The prolific Thomas Mawson (1861–1933), who published the acclaimed first edition of the *Art and Craft of Garden Making* in 1900, cleverly articulated the vocabulary of landscape design so that clients could choose their favourite style of gardening. Through many editions of his book he developed a highly successful practice. At a glance, Peto and Mawson have little in common. Mawson's guide to design enumerates different aspects of garden-making in turn. Whether discussing walls and gates, terraces and steps or ponds and pergolas, it could be read that the purpose of garden design is to combine and relate these features to achieve a harmonising synthesis. Peto, by contrast, and irrespective of the lack of a 'manual of practice', approached a commission with a vision of the associations that the landscape would bring and the memories that it would touch – this is the essence of his poetic sensitivity to form.

Among Peto's contemporaries was Edwin Lutyens, a younger man than him, who worked for a short time in the offices of George and Peto, where his fellow articled pupil, the architect Herbert Baker, described him as full of wit and good stories. In the 1890s, Lutyens formed a successful partnership with Gertrude Jekyll. He was a master of articulating landscape with geometry to grip and direct the eye of the beholder, as he does with particular brilliance at Hestercombe, Folly Farm and Amport House. Lutyens knew Peto and came once to stay with him at Iford Manor in 1914, but history does not record any comments about the garden that he found, nor indeed did Peto leave any critical comments about his or other designers' work. However, some observations suggest that Gertrude Jekyll greatly admired the work of Peto. She sent him copies of her books with affectionate personal dedications, and in her anthologies of *Garden Ornament* (1918 and second edition 1927) she published significantly more of his work than that of Lutyens, often with high praise.

Beginnings at Somerleyton

Harold Ainsworth Peto was born in London on the 11 July 1854, the fifth son of the highly successful builder, engineer and railway contractor Sir Morton Peto, whose country house was Somerleyton Hall, just outside Lowestoft in Suffolk. The house had been extensively rebuilt in the 1840s by Sir Morton to the designs of John Thomas in a medley of Italian and Jacobean styles, with, later in 1852, an enormous Winter Garden (inspired by the Crystal Palace), which

Above: A family gathering: the Peto brothers at Chedington Court, Dorset, in 1915, with Harold standing second from the left.

Left: The colonnade leading to the great terrace at Iford Manor frames the stairway to the King Edward VII column.

sported occasional Moorish details evoking the exotic East. It was here that Harold grew up in a large family of fourteen brothers and sisters, and it is no surprise that his siblings were held in particular affection, and frequently mentioned in his travel diaries. On at least one occasion he accompanied his younger brother and sister around Italy.

At Somerleyton, he may have met the highly successful and prolific garden designer William Nesfield, whose work was dominated by the fashionable revival of the seventeenth-century French parterre, one of which he designed for Sir Morton together with a large hedge maze. Joseph Paxton too, a friend and associate of Sir Morton, was a visitor to Somerleyton where the young Peto could have met him. There are ridge and furrow greenhouses in the kitchen garden made to Paxton's design.

Many of the key events surrounding the success of his father's business ventures – the excitement of such prestigious engineering feats as the first bridge over the St Lawrence River, achieved in spite of the harsh conditions of Canadian winters when building was suspended – were ground-breaking achievements, but many of the great enterprises were completed before Peto was born, or were happening when he was still only a young child. No doubt at a tender age he would have been taken to see the Crystal Palace at Sydenham – that iconic building which housed the Great Exhibition in 1851, designed by Paxton and championed by Sir Morton who gave public and financial support for its

Immaculate Victorian gardens surround Sir Morton Peto's house at Somerleyton Hall, Suffolk, which was Harold's early childhood home.

construction. Such awe-inspiring achievements left Peto with a devotion to his father and family. This was evident in visits to his father, by then an old, ill man living out his days at Cannes, where Peto was pleased to see his parents well housed 'with their lovely view of hills and blue sea' and able sometimes to sit out 'in the open air and gain strength'.

Equally, though, Peto would have suffered the ignominy of the financial failure of Sir Morton's business in the 1860s – an event that may have spawned the thrift and asceticism which were so often found in his lifestyle. When in Venice in 1888 he declared, ' I would rather have only a rag to my back and a piece of art for my soul'. The American collector Isabella Stewart Gardner (who built the Boston Museum at Fenway Court), writing to her friend Bernard Berenson, said she imagined herself at night sleeping like Peto 'with my hair blowing' in the wind. Family anecdote had it that Peto kept Iford without central heating and most visitors found it austere and uncomfortable. He expressed in his American diary of 1887 an admiration for Henry Thoreau's 'plain living and high thinking', and one has to imagine that, rather uncharacteristically, he had read Thoreau's American classic *Walden*.

Among local residents of Lowestoft he might have come across, in his youth at Somerleyton, was the writer Edward Fitzgerald whose chief work was the poetic translation of *The Rubaiyat of Omar Khayyam*, which became a touchstone for the Victorian Romantics with a penchant for titillating tales of the East. Even if Peto never met Fitzgerald, there was a certain sensuality in his nature – so evident in his diaries – which would have been awoken by the pathos evoked in the *Rubaiyat*, that longing for the intoxication of the spirit to carry away all worldly cares. Peto in his Spanish diary wrote of his enjoyment of Irving's *Legends of the Alhambra*, which engendered his longing to visit the Islamic gardens of Andalusia. Sitting in the gardens of the Generalife, his thoughts, recorded in his diary, were wistful as he savoured the moment, much as Omar might have done, but Peto went further and was inspired to obtain an order to visit the garden courts by moonlight. How appropriate then that when he came across an inscription from the *Rubaiyat* when visiting the gardens of Broughton Castle, he copied it down for future reference:

> Yon rising moon that looks for us again
> How oft hereafter will she wax and wane
> How oft hereafter rising look for us
> Through this same garden – and for us in vain

Moving to London

Peto went to Harrow School briefly from 1869 to 1871, where he is recorded as being good at languages. Immediately after leaving school at the age of seventeen, he was apprenticed to a joiner's workshop for nearly a year before entering the practice of the architects J. Clements of Lowestoft. He stayed with them for a year and then moved on to a London architectural firm, Karslake and Mortimers. Two years later, in 1876, Peto went into partnership with Ernest George. Their partnership lasted sixteen years during which time Peto became an Associate of the RIBA, and then was elected a Fellow in 1883, proposed by Ernest George, who wrote in his testimony: 'He has exceptional ability and artistic qualifications for the practice of architecture, knowledge of construction and taste in form and colour.'

George and Peto was one of the most successful London firms – described sometimes as filling a gap between Norman Shaw and Lutyens, working in the Dutch style with colour and tiles. The list of their London projects includes some of the most fashionable and admired of the town houses built during the 1880s. Alongside their commissions in London they were equally active as fashionable country-house builders. There is no documentation that relates what part Peto played in these projects, whether he confined his work to the design of the house or whether he looked at the wider landscape. The Modernist architect S. D. Adshead, when working in the George and Peto office, observed that Ernest George did all the design work, whereas Peto was rarely seen as he spent most of his time with clients. Peto's proficiency as a draughtsman makes this palpably untrue.

It was during the years of his partnership, and in the 1890s before he bought Iford, that Peto wrote some of his most interesting travel diaries. These provide an insight into his personality, his inclinations and obsessions in the arts, his nostalgia and his growing preoccupation with gardens, which became such a potent influence on his future direction. The manuscript diaries for this period are only gradually being published; they are lyrical pieces of writing which have little regard for practical or personal details, such as how he travelled, where he stayed and who he travelled with. Who he wrote the diaries for – his family, his friends or just for himself – is a matter of conjecture. What is

Above: *Harold Peto's drawing room at 7 Collingham Gardens, London, where he lived from 1889–92.*

Above right: *The George and Peto office in Maddox Street, London, c.1887.*

evident, as with many youthful diaries, is his desire to capture his feelings at a particular place and time before they slipped away, to enable him, perhaps, in later life to rekindle those tender yearnings of his youth. No diaries have come to light after 1898, but it is hard to believe that having written so regularly and eloquently in his early years he wrote nothing later.

Travels Abroad: Italy

In April and May of 1887, Peto wrote the first of his lyrical diaries from Italy, where he visited Florence and the Tuscan hill towns. His favourite painters are woven like a golden thread though his daily excursions, and alongside these preoccupations there are jewels of recollection. From his room in Florence looking down on to the Ponte Vecchio and over to Bellosguardo and San Miniato, he heard birdsong: 'To my great and quite unexpected delight I find that bird … is still alive and sings in the mysterious minor key early in the morning which

Left above: *The Villa Medici, Rome, and its gardens were photographed by Charles Latham in the early 1900s. Such Renaissance villas were much in Peto's mind when he was designing villas and gardens on the Riviera.*

Left below: *View from the garden front of the Villa Medici with a bronze statue of Mercury by Giambologna.*

Below: *The south porch to the oval court at the Villa Pia, in the Vatican Gardens, Rome, was the source for the monumental gateways Peto designed to the colonnade at Isola Bella, Cannes.*

charmed me so much before.' We hear him relishing the peaceful moments in his room, full of lilies of the valley and lovely brown-pink roses scenting the room, which has 'such a lovely outlook that I enjoy sitting there as much as anything I do. I am going to sight-see casually; not make a business of it.' He is much taken with the Villa of Lorenzo the Magnificent (Villa at Careggi): 'all round under the eaves runs an external arcaded gallery, carried outside the main wall on corbelled arches – Wisteria in full bloom, climbs right to the most charming Loggia on first floor – open on all three sides – the ceiling looking very rich with frescoes, as I sit in the garden … crimson rhododendrons full out, and a mass of grand colour.' Such descriptions as these bring to mind at once the wisteria at Iford reaching to Peto's bedroom window, and the open loggias on the upper floors of the Riviera villas he was one day to build. He makes just an occasional aside referring to his circle of friends, including a mention of Vernon Lee, and a drive back to Florence, through 'the level evening light', to dine out with Henry James.

Flowers were always with him and he wrote in his diary: 'It is delightful to sit here in this quiet, writing – my morning bunch of tea roses on my knee – 6 perfect soft pink yellow darlings, looking so fresh and sweet, with their leaves all loosely tied together – I am never without flowers in my hand here, from morning to night, in the streets,

looking at pictures, I love to have the presence of these charmers with me.' Flowers were his abiding passion and they became the imperative motive for making a garden. Siena he loved, 'it twines itself round one's heart and the people here have the sweetest, most obliging manners possible, and the women are amazingly handsome …'

America

Peto's first recorded excursion outside Europe was to America in 1887, ten years after he had gone into partnership with Ernest George. From his comments and observations on New York and its architecture, it is clear that he went there to be able to report back at first hand on what was happening in the future premier city of the world. Undoubtedly, he was encouraged or even sent as a special envoy by George, in the hope that knowledge gained in America would help the business. His search for modern developments and particular features makes this diary very different from all the others. Atypically, he applied himself to all the practical details, referring to sanitation and heating, as well as making a close scrutiny of different materials used in interior decoration.

One of the fashionable houses he visited was that of the New York financier and art collector Henry Marquand, who became President of the Metropolitan Museum of Art. Peto was shown round by Marquand, and described with guarded admiration the art treasures in rooms of every style – Japanese, Moorish, English Renaissance – but he was particularly struck by the 'wonderful' grand piano designed for Marquand by the Victorian painter Alma-Tadema, though he seems even more impressed by the price, exclaiming, 'it cost 47,000 dollars!' He appears to have had endless introductions to rich and famous families, including the Vanderbilts, Conklings and Astors. He was shown all the latest technology: elevators, steam heating, ventilation, pneumatic tubes for messages, and 'the buildings in the business parts like mountains above you, 11 & 12 stories high!' He admired Central

Above: *The main axis at the Villa d'Este, Tivoli, Pirro Ligorio's Renaissance masterpiece built for Cardinal Ippolito d'Este. Photographed by Charles Latham c.1901.*

Right above: *The Medici Villa at Careggi, near Florence, with its upper-storey loggia described so evocatively by Peto in his Italian diary, 1887.*

Right below: *One of the twin pavilions, known as the Loggias of the Muses, in the upper court of the Villa Lante, Bagnaia.*

Park ('most cleverly laid out') and referred to the 'transparent air' in contrast to the smoke and choking air of London. 'Why', he asked, 'should London be rendered filthy and foul by pouring out its smoke', and noted that in New York they only burned anthracite.

Little glimpses into the social life of New York amused him sufficiently to put them on record. He was intrigued by Mrs Astor who had a box at the opera and told him, 'I always go from 9–11. I don't care whether the prima Donna is dying or what is happening – when I leave I go away exactly at 11.' He travelled to Washington, of course, visited the White House, Philadelphia, and then went north to Boston, where, with an introduction from Henry James, he was entertained by the formidable Mrs Jack Gardner and accompanied by the painter John Singer Sargent – later Peto was to collect many Italian art works for Gardner's Renaissance palazzo, Fenway Court. He visited the Niagara Falls, where he described the water, 'all swirling and tossing as if in an overpowering passion, and seething in a way I never saw water do before', and on to Quebec for 'sleighing and tobogganing'. He was not disappointed, spending, it seems, days on the tobogganing slide travelling at 'ferocious speeds as covered with ½ inch of ice! Steering almost impossible.' This was the youthful Peto, full of *joie de vivre*, with high excitement and enjoyment of the escapades of youth, and it speaks of his spirit of adventure, his thrill at taking things on. He was not a stuffy Victorian, but very much a young man breathing with life.

Above: *Peto's drawing of the Charles V pavilion, which was also the inspiration for the garden house at Ilnacullin.*

Left (top): *The garden house at Isola Bella, Cannes, was based on the Charles V pavilion in the Alcázar gardens in Seville* (centre).

Left: *The Court of the Canal (*Patio de la Acequia*) in the gardens of the Generalife, Granada, photographed in 1916.*

This early photograph, taken in 1898, of the Court of the Canal in the gardens of the Generalife, Granada, with cypresses along the canal, shows it as Peto would have seen it.

Spain

The following year Peto travelled to Spain, leaving London in April and revelling in the trip south, as from day to day the sun became warmer. He lets us know right at the start of his diary that he has longed to visit the 'East', which he plans to do when his boat reaches Gibraltar: 'I have long wished to get a peep at the gorgeous East and I believe Tangiers is a good specimen …' At 'Gib', he gives us an account of his early morning stroll along the Alameda. The description of his experience is evocative and sensual and shows a keen interest in the plants that surrounded him: 'a sort of long undulating shady garden full of great stone pines, palms with their dates on, oleanders, pomegranates with their scarlet flowers, figs, bamboos, cypresses, bananas, ilex and acacia in full bloom making the whole place redolent; the most charming undergrowth of Aruncus in masses, roses, heliotropes, marguerites, white, yellow and pied, nasturtium climbing everywhere and the stern grey sweep of great aloes and cactus; everything bathed with the tropical rain of last night, the birds singing everywhere, and butterflies

hovering among the flowers.' He was later thrilled by his 'peep' at the East, crossing over to Morocco and describing the bustling life of the town of Tangiers in contrast to the oasis of peace within the old Moorish gardens. This contrast must have struck Gertrude Jekyll, too, as she chose to illustrate some of the enclosed gardens of Algeria in *Garden Ornament* (1918).

In Seville, Peto described the gardens of the Alcázar as a 'paradise', 'Oranges on all sides in full bloom, the air is quite intoxicating … I now feel the charm of *water* in the garden running and spouting on all sides.' No wonder then that the first thing he did at Iford was to tap into the springs on the hillside so that water could run to every corner of the garden, and assuredly water became a dominant theme in many of his commissions. He drew particular attention to the Charles V pavilion 'lined inside and out with incised and coloured tiles and surrounded with a colonnade, a fountain in the centre.' He made a small sketch of this building that later was to become the inspiration for the garden house at Ilnacullin.

Peto was never without roses: 'The nice gardener has brought me *such* a lovely bunch of pale yellow Niphetos roses from the balcony of

Maria de Padilla's window.' He was much taken with Spanish singing and dancing and after hearing some excellent musicians he arranged a private party for himself. 'They danced and sang alternately till 5 and taught me how to play the castanets and we all enjoyed it very much … all sorts of dances – Seguidillas, Cachuchas, Manchegas, Malagueñas, Boleras, and one from Havana. The acacia in full blossom close up to the windows and orange groves close by and the gardens full of roses and great French poppies in full bloom and in the intervals of the soup and dances the nightingales sang till I felt it a desecration for anything to interrupt them.'

It was Peto's visit to Granada and the Alhambra that charmed him beyond all else, and his memories of garden courts full of roses and little canals beside cool pavilions were to prove indelible and would nurture his creative spirit. He recalled this vision often in his future designs and the elements were reworked in different ways to become the key features of many of his gardens. When he arrived at Granada in the late afternoon he was impatient to have his first glimpse of the Court of the Canal (*Patio de la Acequia*), a scene that he had obviously anticipated from written accounts. He took a rest 'under a cool Moorish arcade, outside open to a prim court with a rushing stream of water along the centre, with cut myrtle hedges and masses of roses.' He described the orange trees, the pale monthly roses and the 'rude brown towers' each with 'a different miracle of loveliness … like a lovely flower or fruit enclosed in a rugged rind, giving no hint of the beauties contained within.' This last metaphor so appealed to him that when years later he was planning the cloister at Iford he wanted it to be like that – simple and unadorned on the outside with all the richness hidden inside.

He described his moments of inactivity to give the most vivid and complete picture of a longed-for contentment: 'Daily I perch myself in a comfortable corner on a parapet under the great mass of the Torre de la Vela where is the loveliest of gardens filled with tea and other roses of the greatest beauty, thousands and thousands of blossoms (which they let me pick what I want of, so I live in the scent of luscious roses day and night).' He spent hours walking round the Alhambra by day and even moonlight, and took note of 'lovely little terraced and trellised gardens tucked away in obscure corners'. These 'perfect pictures' he would later recall and use at home – possibly in the Rose Garden at Crichel, Dorset. His diary finished in Madrid where he visited the Prado, and, apart from appreciating the Velázquez paintings, he observed that, 'Native art was not born here till early religious feeling

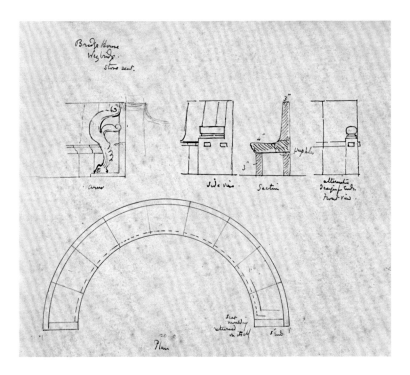

Top: *Peto's plan for the seat at Bridge House, Surrey, shows alternative forms for the ends.*

Above: *The carved stone exedra of the priestess Mamia, in Pompeii, inspired many of Peto's own designs for semicircular seats.*

Left: *Peto's designs for semicircular seats were used in many of his gardens, including this one at Hinton Admiral, Hampshire.*

was gone.' However, he was full of praise for Spanish armour and metalwork, and this helps to account for his use of Spanish iron gates which he procured for his clients – they were often his preference in the garden, in contrast to solid wooden gates. He saw them as defining the space, while at the same time giving a taste of what lay ahead – ironwork was less of a barrier than a wooden gate. It is clear from many of these descriptions and comments that Peto's Spanish experience was one of the most formative for his future creative period.

Greece

During the 1880s, Peto was busy in his partnership with Ernest George, which was mainly centred on London, where he was living, though his travel diaries hint at a slowly emerging distaste for his life in London and signs of an overwhelming desire to leave and live a life in the country, above all with a garden. Just a year before he took the decision to leave the partnership at the age of thirty-eight, he was travelling in Greece and there were strong signs that his mind was almost made up. On 'a true Athenian day', as he called it, with 'dazzling sun and bright elastic air like champagne', the contrast between this situation and what he remembered of London must have stung his resolve: 'Oh for freedom not to go back to the vile choking depraved town! As soon as ever I can see my way to the most modest competency I will cut it for ever.' Later on the same trip, when he moves north to Turkey, he sits in 'a modest little garden', in which he had been made welcome by the owner, overlooking the Bosphorus and the tiny Therapia Bay. With a simple scene around him of roses and white stocks and wisteria running along the iron railings, he begins a heart-rending lament for a garden: 'Shall I *never* be able to compass my very modest ambition in respect of a small spot in the country where I can grow my flowers and each morning come out in the freshness of the new day and tend them and see the growth and changes since yesterday?' He then moderates this sudden *cri de coeur* with a sobering thought: 'For years I have longed for it and to escape that to me hateful life in London, I must try and be more economical I suppose and so make it possible, though town is so detestable in my eyes that it is only possible to endure it with heaps of flowers and music etc!'

As his Greek diary unfolds there are, from time to time, little glimpses of scenes that jog the memory and catch the imagination. When he was on Corfu walking on the cliffs overlooking the 'dazzling blue sea', he spied a ruined temple beneath him built right on the edge of the cliffs – this momentary vision was to reappear in the temple at Ilnacullin which stands out on a promontory, with the sea below and the mountains beyond. While still on Corfu, in the north of the island, he visited the Palæokastritsa convent – an old castle built high on the rocky coast. These scenes and others by the sea became vivid and lasting memories that were to stimulate his vision for the island garden in Ireland and the Cap Ferrat villas on the Riviera. It was Greek architecture that made the impact that held his imagination. On the Acropolis he exclaims: 'What a revelation of beauty and fitness it is, how impossible to know anything about Athenian architecture from seeing it anywhere else.' And at the same time, comparisons are inevitable as his disgust for London, which lurks behind his thoughts,

grows: 'It is a severe wrench to one's mind even to recall for a moment such sorrowful grimy state of atmosphere as has reduced the fine British Museum to the blackest and most dismal object.'

A Move to the Country

In the following summer of 1892, Peto brought his partnership with Ernest George to an end (the deed of dissolution of the partnership was dated 31 October); it was a perfectly amicable and businesslike parting. George agreed to dissolve the agreement on the basis that Peto would no longer practise architecture in Britain. This arrangement was complied with, apparently willingly, as it is likely that Peto already had it in mind to work on landscape architecture. As the agreement only pertained to Britain, he knew he was free to create an architectural practice abroad. Almost immediately, in the autumn of 1892, he moved out of London and lived for a few years at Hernden House in Kent (now known as Heronden). It is possible to conjecture that at this stage he was thinking of being near the Channel ports for easy access to boats for the Continent. Although he carried out some minor alterations around the house, placed some of his favourite architectural sculptures in the garden and was visited by some of his long-standing friends, like Isabella Gardner from Boston, he did not stay very long (writing later to Mrs Gardner that he felt his stay was only temporary). He left Kent at the end of 1895, and moved to Landford House near Salisbury in the spring of 1896.

Peto's move could have been made for personal reasons, as in 1893 his eldest brother, Sir Henry, had bought Chedington Court, Dorset, which subsequently became a sort of 'family seat', and many of the family were buried in the churchyard there. Landford House belonged to his eldest sister, who wanted to live in London, which meant the house was free for Peto to look after. It was also quite central for southern England, where many of his later commissions were carried out, and close to Southampton for regular trips to the Continent.

Travels Again

In these intervening years between finishing with the partnership in London and finally settling at Iford in 1899, Peto travelled extensively: Egypt, Sicily, Venice, Germany, Brittany and, most often, southern France and northern Italy, as well as taking an around the world trip in 1898, during which he spent much time in Japan. It is a matter of conjecture whether he carried out any garden design during this period – nothing firm has emerged. The dates of his major commissions show that he was extremely busy from 1900 onwards until the outbreak of the First World War, with many projects running in parallel as no doubt his reputation spread.

Sicily and Egypt

The accounts of Peto's major trips after 1892 reveal that his enthusiasm for plants and gardens was the motivating force behind his choice of

travel destination. Whereas the major Italian trips during the 1880s had been inspired by his excitement at visiting churches, museums and seeing works of art, his accounts of his subsequent journeys show that he viewed the landscape and gardens with a new interest and was preoccupied with drawing and committing to memory designs and

Left: *The wisteria arbour in Prince Horita's garden in Tokyo, photographed for the* Country Life *articles on the gardens of Japan in 1901.*

Above: *View of a private garden in Yokohama.*

Below: *A stepping-stone bridge in Prince Horita's garden, Tokyo.*

plants. He looked at the landscape as he had looked at paintings, observing the thread of history, keen to make a living connection. This is evident when, visiting the ruins of the Greek city of Agrigento in Sicily in April 1895, in a moment of repose gazing out to sea he noted, 'For a scene to touch me most deeply it must have a *historic* feeling about it, the knowledge and visible signs that men have loved it and made the most of it in times gone by.' It was evidently Greek culture that inspired him, for he contrasts his feelings for Sicily with his experience in Algiers, where he felt no inclination to write about it because its past 'belonged to pirates whose only history was cursed by every one who heard of them.' His interest in history evolved from the civilising aspects of culture and the sense of place which it generates: 'I love the feeling that others have loved a spot and perhaps made gardens of part, and then to come long afterwards, alone, and quietly drink in that matchless feeling of it all, is *most* delightful.'

There are signs already in his Sicilian diary that he was beginning to tire of travelling, not that he was tired of new countries and new scenes, but it was the wearying journeys that he began to resent. He records for his future guidance that 'the pleasures are not worth the pains'. He had felt that it was all worth it when he was escaping from London and the business, but by now his circumstances were different, living in the country with a garden he loved. 'This moving', he wrote, 'seems to me a succession of miseries – trains crowded, dreadfully hot, or so late', and 'an hour's anxiety trying to get done what I had to do.'

Although Peto was no longer in London, he still remembered it with horror: first, in the period just after leaving the partnership in October 1892, then on his Nile trip in December and January when he declared his thoughts about that 'hateful London winter', which he recalled so vividly, with 'the endless dreary cold stinky blackness, stretching away in the past and the future'. And again, travelling through Austria, on one of his undated later excursions in the 1890s, he compared what he found with what he had left behind in London: 'I *nowhere* see that vile hopeless sodden slovenliness that at every corner and every turn greets you in London.' By contrast in Vienna, 'One sees delightful gardens tastefully laid out and beautifully kept and watered and endless seats for those who cannot pay and music at every turn for them to listen to.'

Japan

Peto's final long trip was around the world to Japan, in 1898, for which the record of his journey survives; it is the most revealing of all about his interest in gardens and particularly plants. At every stage he sought out nurseries and visited specialist growers. Particularly informative for this purpose was his visit to the iris growers at Hori-Kiri, which he describes as the 'Mecca of the iris-growing', and tells us how they are cultivated: 'I came to see the spot and how they grow it; on little promontories and islands [and] among the iris tanks are charming little thatched open sheds from which to "view" the flowers ... and raised walks lead about among the pools.' He carefully made a note of a bank of *sibirica* and the Kaempfer iris, both of which were to feature in his later garden designs. This combination of flowers and water must particularly have appealed to him. Some other plants also get a special mention, such as the wonderful paeony garden in Kyoto, which 'absolutely took my breath away'. His observation of wild flowers is just as keen: 'It is interesting to find nearly all the wild flowers in Japan are old garden favourites, Cydonia, chrysanthemum, wisteria, Bocconia, *Iris fimbriata*, cherry, plum, Kerria, camellia, hydrangea, spiraea, deutzia, azaleas, *Lilium auratum*, etc. – a curious dearth of herbaceous wild flowers.' He was not only observing the plants, for he was actively

visiting nurseries and arranging to have plants sent back to England. No wonder he needed a garden back at home to grow them all in.

He comments on the Japanese style of gardening and draws parallels with Europe: 'There is something very attractive about these gardens; of course they are entirely of the "natural garden" type .... The gardens, as everything else here, are a question of form rather than colour ... our charming "flower garden" does not exist here.' He had not seen anything that he called 'Great Art', a term which he reserved for the Greeks, for though he admired the Japanese decorative arts – drawing, carving and metalwork which he extolled 'beyond all praise' – in summing up his experiences, he said: 'I do not leave Japan with the tugging at my heart strings, which I feel on leaving Italy.' Most enlightening is a prophetic remark he made in Hong Kong before his return journey across the Pacific: 'Decidedly I will never undertake a *long* journey again; it is not worth it .... Far wiser to stay mostly *at home* and "cultivate your garden".' Which indeed was the direction his life was now to take.

Iford Manor: Home at Last

It is quite probable that Peto had already discovered Iford before he left England, for later he recalls in *The Boke of Iford* that after discovering the Manor it took him some time to decide to purchase it, mainly, he said, because the estate was much larger and more expensive than he could afford at the time. He had been looking out to buy a small manor house for a while, as he records in a letter to Mrs Gardner in 1896, saying, 'I have seen scores, but they all have some fatal objection.' And in the same letter he declares his purpose: 'It would be a pleasure to me to devote myself to really making the most beautiful garden I could as a worthy setting to a charming old house.'

Although perhaps at first Peto had 'fatal objections' to Iford, he must have soon come round to it, for he bought the property and moved into it early in 1899, just six months after his return from the Far East. His

Above left: *This canal in the 'Dutch' garden at Westbury Court, Gloucestershire, is focused on a Classical-style pavilion. This was an arrangement used in a number of Peto's gardens.*
Above: *The Jacobean balustrade on the terrace at The Hall, Bradford-on-Avon, is very similar to the one Peto used in the garden at Petwood, Lincolnshire.*

Peto liked the honey-coloured Ham Hill stone used to build Montacute House, Somerset, and specified it for many of his commissions. The pool with a balustrade, constructed in the nineteenth century, is the focal point of the large Elizabethan garden.

travels after this remain a matter of conjecture, though his trips to the Riviera must have been frequent as his architectural practice grew around Cannes on the Côte d'Azur during the Edwardian period. It is surprising that no diary records of these years have come to light. Perhaps they were never written, which suggests that the potent desire to record those moments of youthful pleasure became submerged in a more stable middle age, when his practice used most of his energy.

The Working Years and After

The majority of Harold Peto's major commissions were begun after 1900 and largely completed before 1914; doubtless he continued to supervise and advise on some of his major projects after the War, but the evidence of new work is very sketchy. Dating these commissions is difficult, too, because several of them were ongoing over many years. Bridge House must be one of the earliest, with advice given by Peto at least from 1900 onwards, then Easton Lodge and Hartham from 1903, Buscot Park 1904, Heale House, Crichel and Hinton Admiral from 1906, High Wall, Petwood, Ilnaculllin and West Dean from 1910,

and Parkfield (Witanhurst) 1913. There were also small projects for family members: his sisters Helen, at Wayford Manor, and Sarah, at Burton Pynsent. He developed his practice on the Riviera during this period as well, building at least five large villas and gardens, and advising on and designing gardens for others. His practice in the South of France was so popular that he remarked in a letter to the heir of the West Dean estate, Edward James, that Cap Ferrat was known locally as 'Peto Point'.

There are a host of other gardens in Britain on which Peto may have worked; from their style that is certainly credible, although there is no firm documentation to support this. One of the most striking examples is at Sedgwick Park in Sussex, where George and Peto had been commissioned to make additions and alterations to the house in 1886 for Robert Henderson, Director of the Bank of England. Later work was done on the house in 1903 and 1904. The gardens could well have been designed by Peto, with canals, framing hedges, balustrades and terraces – typical features of his work – but there is no documentary evidence. At Glencot near Wells, Somerset, the partners built a new country house in 1887. The garden has a bridge over a small stream, with a saintly figure, perhaps St Cuthbert, dominating the parapet, as Britannia would later do on the bridge at Iford Manor; it is

uncannily in the mode of Peto, with the date 1901 on the parapet. Also at Glencot, there is a spring surrounded by a curious architectural stone frame, which immediately recalls some of the Pompeian fountains – features from the Roman world were to figure prominently in Peto's later work.

It comes as some surprise that as well as garden-making Peto was passionately keen on interior design, which he developed for his clients in the villas on the Riviera. He also received the prestigious commission to design the first-class accommodation on the *Mauretania*, sister ship to the ill-fated *Lusitania* which was tragically sunk off Ireland in 1915. Peto's designs for the *Mauretania* in 1907 were widely acclaimed, and the ship held the coveted Blue Riband for the fastest Atlantic crossings until 1929.

During the war years Peto must have felt driven to reflect on his achievements and specifically chose to make a written record of that central theme of his life, the making of Iford. He employed a calligrapher to transcribe his words to create a beautiful medieval-style manuscript, which was bound together, accompanied by photographs, in a handsome, tooled leather binding, which he called *The Boke of Iford*. The book survives as a statement of his views on garden-making and to some extent as a history of Iford Manor.

The circumstances of many of Peto's clients were changed by the War. Society had undergone a major upheaval that left few with the appetite to revive those halcyon days when the creation of gardens was in the forefront of country pursuits. The taste for making such gardens had for most withered away and there is no evidence that Peto continued with new commissions. From the little material we have from the 1920s it is evident that Peto continued to travel regularly to the Continent, no doubt much of it for pleasure, but quite possibly to provide further advice to his clients on the Riviera. By the end of the decade, he was in poor health, but regularly visited at Iford by his family, particularly by his brother Basil, his closest sisters living in Somerset and his dear friends. Even near the end of his life when journeys would have been difficult he longed to travel again to his 'beloved city' Venice. He died at Iford Manor on Easter Day 1933.

Above: A rare glimpse of Harold Peto at home, sitting on the newly built seat at the western end of the great terrace at Iford Manor, photographed in 1907.

Right: The great terrace at Iford Manor, Wiltshire. Peto's vision for this may have been the determining factor in his decision to purchase the house in 1899.

1:
Rotundas
and
Pergolas

Petwood, Lincolnshire: (above) *The garden house was a prerequisite for most Edwardian gardens, and Peto gave full rein to a delightful array of designs.*

Easton Lodge, Essex: (left) *Peto's Renaissance style was nowhere more evident than here. Beyond the terrace, the roof of Lady Warwick's tree house is just discernible in the branches of an enormous oak.*

Whereas horticulture and colourful bedding were for the Victorians defining characteristics of their gardens, for the Edwardians it was garden architecture. The Victorian preoccupation with bedding displays on a vast scale, together with the dextrous ingenuity of the French parterre, were abandoned, notably under the influence of the Arts and Crafts architects, in favour of a revivalism of the old formal style, which had its demise during the eighteenth-century landscape movement. The old formalism relied much more on structure than it did on horticultural expertise; hence the criticism of the new architect-gardeners by the doyen of horticulture at the time, William Robinson (1838–1935). The structures were many and varied and not by any means all related to Tudor English gardens – Elizabethan knots for example were seldom featured. It was very often the smaller scale and intimacy of the early gardens, in essence the old English manor garden with walled areas around the house, which so charmed the would-be garden architects of the Edwardian period.

Some structures in particular that became so fashionable after 1900, such as pergolas, rotundas and temples, were not features of early English gardens. 'Pergola' became a universal word for the different types of walk-through structures that were popularised, particularly,

through the works of Robinson and the landscape architect Thomas Mawson. These structures were quickly recognised as being ideally suited for flowering climbing plants and became a *sine qua non* for garden lovers. The word and the basic construction derive, of course, from Italy where the pergola was used as a practical means of training vines. In England, the bower-like structures that were so often part of the old pleasance and are equivalent to the pergola were called arbours; universally, the arbour was constructed with a rounded, arched roof. Two pergolas in Italy that became archetypes for the Edwardian versions were the simple wooden pergola in Frederic Eden's garden in Venice and the stone-pillared one at Amalfi. Both were illustrated in William Robinson's *The English Flower Garden* (1889 and 1893 editions). As Mrs Eden was Gertrude Jekyll's sister it is not surprising that Jekyll early on saw the potential of the utilitarian pergola for use as a decorative support for flowering climbers in the English garden.

Above left: *Château de Chantilly, France: The pavilion on the Ile d'Amour was described by Gertrude Jekyll as 'a remarkable example of elaborate French treillage.' Peto had visited Chantilly, and structures like this were an inspiration for the* treillage *pergola at Easton Lodge, Essex.*

Above right: *A seventeenth-century* treillage *design by Jean Le Pautre.*

Harold Peto copied the Amalfi pergola and its position overlooking the sea when he began his practice designing villas and gardens for his clients on the Riviera. Similar versions of this pergola became the key design for his gardens at West Dean, Sussex, and High Wall, Oxfordshire, both constructed with supporting uprights and cross beams running from column to column: a trabeated structure. For the pedant or purist it is ill fitting to call the *treillage* arbour at Easton Lodge, Essex, a pergola, but so pervasive was this term in the Edwardian era that contemporaneous sources all refer to these magnificent structures as that. The West Dean pergola is a fine example of the true pergola structure and in essence more typical of the period.

Classically inspired rotundas or temples are not particularly a hallmark of the early twentieth century, nor of the early English garden. Pavilions, summerhouses and banqueting houses, as opposed to temples, all occur in earlier periods, but without doubt the summerhouse, like the pergola, belonged to the cherished gardens of Edward VII's reign. Greek and Roman temples were observed by travellers on the Grand Tour and it was in the eighteenth century that they became a familiar feature of the landscape garden. Harold Peto was one of the few architects who revived them in the early twentieth century, and used them in a simple way, as an eye-catcher, in many of his gardens.

Duncombe Park, Yorkshire: (above) *The rotunda was a feature of many eighteenth-century landscape parks. This photograph was published in* Country Life *in 1905.*

Montacute House, Somerset: (below) *The fountain basin, photographed in 1898. Although taking much of its ornamental design from the Elizabethan forecourt, is in fact nineteenth-century. The balustraded pool at Easton Lodge, Essex, is strikingly similar.*

EASTON LODGE, ESSEX

Of Peto's early commissions, Easton Lodge for the Countess of Warwick must have been one of the most prestigious, and its scale gave him the opportunity to draw on his favourite themes: the pergolas, the lily pool, the Italian Garden and even a Japanese Garden (or 'Jap' garden as he always referred to them) by the lake. And more. To each of these areas he was able to bring such breadth of expression as to make the lily pool the central focus of a magnificent sunk garden surrounded by retaining walls, with six flights of wide steps. It also included his favourite curved seats flanked by columns, and a pair of grand pergolas designed with all the bravura of the most carefully wrought seventeenth-century French *treillage*. The scene by the lake with a Japanese tea-house, complete with statues of Japanese attendants, harked back to his recent journey to Japan, where his abiding delight had been taking tea overlooking the lake, with the wisteria reaching out over the water. Not to be forgotten is the Countess's magnificent tree house positioned high up in the spreading boughs of a great oak, with views down the pleached lime avenues and over the lily pool.

It has been suggested that the garden was commissioned from Peto around 1902, although his earliest sketches for the garden are dated 1903. The mansion of Easton Lodge stood in the middle of an historic estate which had been in the Maynard family since Elizabethan times, and in 1865 the young Frances Evelyn became the sole heiress when she was only four years old. The house was built on slightly rising ground surrounded at the time by parkland, which, according to descriptions from the Edwardian era, was planted with fine groups of oak, hornbeam and Scotch fir. As far back as the eighteenth century, engravings show the great avenues with the *patte d'oie* focusing the viewer's attention on the house. While she was living at the nearby house of Stone Hall, Frances early on showed her interest in garden-making – the gardens she created there appeared in *Some English Gardens*, published in 1904, by Jekyll and Elgood – so it is not surprising that she wanted to make the garden at Easton a suitable setting for social gatherings.

At some time in the 1890s, the Countess had become the favourite of the future Edward VII and was known in his circle as 'Darling Daisy'. The Prince of Wales and his entourage were frequent visitors to Easton, and it is significant that Peto should write on one of his sketches for Easton, 'Plan of small Sat to Monday Villa garden', conjuring up the picture of those idyllic parties (on what today is 'the weekend'). Around 1900, the Countess embraced socialism, becoming known for her outright sympathy with 'the least fortunate in society', and then to the dismay of many in the English aristocracy she began to entertain Fabians, the new politicians of the working class and

Daisy, Countess of Warwick's nineteenth-century Jacobean-style mansion is the backdrop to the Victorian terrace where a semicircle of deserted seats conjures up wistful scenes of long-gone social gatherings.

the trades union movement. It is therefore totally understandable, although for some quite ironic, that she employed the Salvation Army to dig the sunken garden and the sumptuous lily pond, which was to become the centrepiece of the great Italian feature.

The 'colonists' as they were called were housed in temporary accommodation at Easton after being 'rescued' from the streets of London. Lady Warwick caused outrage, as she did on many occasions, in the local community, who feared that ex-drunkards and convicts would corrupt the neighbourhood. According to *The Social Gazette* in 1903, the work was carried out during wintertime and included landscaping the Italian Garden, the Japanese Garden, formal lawns and walks. We are told the 'army of men' took just five months to complete it. The Countess, it is said, was well pleased, stating that: 'The work and conduct of the men have justified the experiment far beyond my highest expectations.' After the main earthworks were completed one assumes that contractors were called in to carry out the huge task of assembling and building the retaining walls, steps, balustrades and lily pond to finish what became one of the finest gardens of the period.

The formal area that Peto designed covers at least 5 acres, and up to 20 acres if the lake and Japanese Garden are included. It was all laid out to the north of the Victorian mansion on ground sloping gently away from the house. The prospect, to say the least, lacked interest, so Peto seized the chance, gaining added height and drama with the framing pergolas. Beyond them the sunk garden also relieved the monotony of the even ground. There were already some fine specimen trees on the lawn in front of the house, including a large cedar of Lebanon, a catalpa and a Tree of heaven (*Ailanthus altissima*). On this lawn there were four square beds – the 'geometric flower garden' as it was referred to in the *Gardener's Magazine* of 1907 – with raised stone kerbs, each of which had a vase on a pedestal in the centre. From early photographs and accounts they were annually planted

Above: The society lady, the Countess of Warwick, as she appeared in Country Life *in 1901, looking remarkably beautiful at the age of forty.*

Right: The cross axis from pergola to pergola separates the Victorian terrace from the games' lawn. This view down the Long Alley between sentinel yews is terminated at the east end by a curved stone seat with its companion table.

with the Victorians' favourite bedding plants: petunias, geraniums and salvias. They form a scheme that does not fit easily into our notion of Peto's planting, and indeed there is no evidence that Peto designed them – rather heavy and Victorian for him – but nevertheless he would have thought their style provided an appropriate setting for the mansion. There is a delightful photographic record of the extent of the wide shady lawns spread with the best of the garden seats from the Pyghtle Works at Bedford (then the foremost supplier of garden furniture and ornaments): a scene for which it is easy to imagine the soirées held beneath the boughs of the Heavenly tree.

Beyond the lawn and running at right angles to the main axis of the garden – the axis that runs all the way from the house to the sunk garden – is the tightly clipped yew alley, or Green Walk, stretching right across the formal area. At the eastern end, the yew hedge was planted in a perfect semicircle to make the setting for one of Peto's favourite stone seats based on the Roman model. Peto was to use these seats often as key features to terminate a vista. In the recess of the stone seat he designed an octagonal stone table, very similar to the ones he did for Iford and Hinton Admiral. On summer evenings shafts of sunlight would have reached down the alley to the perfect place to sit and contemplate the passing day; as if to confirm this the young Lady Warwick was photographed sitting on the seat accompanied by her favourite hounds. The view down the Green Walk was lined with fastigiate yews placed on the walk like waiting sentinels. The other end of the alley, leading to the Rose Garden, is unenclosed, but marked by a pedestal sundial with an octagonal base; it was drawn by Peto in February 1903, with the instructions that it was to be 4-feet high and intended for a statue.

The rosery, formed in a large area to the west of the main garden, is surrounded by evergreen hedges and shrubs and was planted, according to a contemporary source, with an abundance of roses – between 6,000 and 7,000 plants in an endless diversity of colouring. Gravel walks divided the turf areas in which variously shaped beds had been cut. Hybrid perpetuals seem to have been the most largely

Left: *Finely turned wooden Classical columns, architraves and roof trusses stretch the length of this complex seventeenth-century-style* treillage. *The arched roofs are covered with jute netting to support a profusion of climbers and rambling roses.*

Below: *The generous scale of this magnificent pergola, with its central dome and spacious side entrances, can be clearly appreciated here. The* treillage *is smothered in climbing plants, but openings between the columns and circular windows frame views over the central tennis and croquet lawns, and the gardens on either side.*

grown, with the principal aim of colour massing, while dark yews encircled this part of the garden to show off the monthly roses. (Now rather more prosaically described as 'repeat flowering').

The alley is a place to linger before striking off in different directions; it makes the transition between the open, picturesque planting on the lawns in front of the house and the large rectangular sunk croquet lawn, flanked by symmetrical pergolas shaded with roses and other climbers. Paths run through the pergolas with windows on to the central lawns and then emerge on a second cross axis, linking pergola to pergola along the length of the lily pool, with views over the Italian Garden and back to the house over the croquet lawn. This kind of pergola was the most magnificent of any created in this period, taking its style and character from the intricate *treillage* of French seventeenth-century gardens. The *treillage* designs of that earlier period, being made entirely of wood, have long been lost to us. However, in Edwardian times there was clearly a desire to revive the feature, but in a less elaborate form; examples were included in Mawson's book on garden-making and the Pyghtle Works incorporated a number of designs in their catalogue. A glance at most of these shows that they were generally of a light construction, relatively small in scale and provided only a rather theatrical backdrop for garden climbers. They were the forerunners of the ephemeral garden trellis. It appears that Peto's designs were drawn from late-seventeenth-century examples, such as at Chantilly, which he had definitely visited, and were later illustrated in Jekyll's *Garden Ornament* (1918). He also looked at the work of the early-eighteenth-century French architect Jacques-François Blondel in *De la distribution des Maisons de Plaisance* (1738) and redrew some fine plates, one of which he used for a trellis screen at Bridge House.

At Easton Lodge each pergola is some 120-feet long, constructed with wooden columns and carved Ionic capitals supporting a moulded architrave over which run segmental, curvilinear trusses carrying the running purlins. Each column is supported on a dado some 3-feet high, with trelliswork running between them. The structure is pierced by two large openings giving access to the croquet lawn, and is crowned at its centre with a dome and finial. From photographs of the time, it appears that the entire structure was covered in netting to provide extra support for climbing plants, and there was general agreement that 'Mr. H. A. Peto has fully appreciated the special advantages of wood construction', (*Country Life*, 1909). Already by 1907, judging from contemporary photographs, the structures were swathed in roses, many of them named in the *Gardener's Magazine* in 1907: 'Lady Gay', 'Dorothy Perkins', 'Crimson Rambler', 'Aimée Vibert', 'Felicité Perpetué', varieties that formed 'an excellent selection for such purposes'. Other climbers, including wisteria, polygonums, clematis and Virginia creeper are all referred to in the *Gardeners' Chronicle* in 1913, and from the photographs and horticultural

At the heart of the sunk garden, the balustraded Italian pool forms the pivotal point. The dense planting surrounding the beds softens the geometric forms, while retaining walls support a panoply of climbers and ramblers. The pergola is in the distance over the tennis lawn.

survivals it is evident that *Periploca graeca* (Silk vine) and Russian vine were also growing freely over the trelliswork.

However magnificent the pergolas, the *pièce de resistance* at Easton must be the balustraded lily pond, which forms the central feature of the sunk Italian Garden. The pool is over 100-feet long, forming a broad canal with apsidal ends; the continuity of the balustrade is interrupted at the mid-point on each side to allow immediate access to the water. These openings could even be landing stages for a small boat that would push out in summer between the profusion of lilies. It was the sensitive Peto at work: he wanted us to appreciate this beautiful access to the water with a little *frisson*. He did something similar at Heale House, where a small quay was constructed right at the edge of the chalk stream. But it is not only the water he wanted us to appreciate: Peto loved feeding the goldfish in Japan, so this could have been the feeding stage, and equally he loved watching the trout dart through the current at Heale.

The pool at Easton has often been compared to the one at Montacute, which undoubtedly would have been familiar to Peto. Montacute was designed and constructed in the mid-nineteenth century and occupied the focal point of the large Elizabethan garden. Comparisons of the two pools show immediately that the balusters surrounding the one at Montacute have the swelling towards the base, while the ones at Easton have symmetrical swellings to either side of a central bead. Much more fruitful is to compare the style of the Elizabethan balustrade which surrounds the forecourt at Montacute. The whole – the design of the balusters, the coping and the intermediate pillars to either side of each section of the balustrade – is a very similar pattern and it is much more credible to imagine that Peto was using the Elizabethan balustrade when he was designing the lily pool for Lady Warwick. Moreover, the material chosen for the Italian Garden at Easton was the beautiful honey-coloured stone quarried at

Above: *Peto's sketch for the Japanese tea-house. The photograph shows that his design was followed closely.*

Right: *Lady Warwick embraced all kinds of gardening styles, and, inspired by his travels to Japan, Peto designed this Japanese tea-house on the lake. It is sited well beyond the Italian Garden, and projects far out from the shore. Tea would have been taken almost completely surrounded by water, with wisteria cascading from the roof beams.*

Ham Hill in Somerset and used to build Montacute and its garden features between 1599 and 1602.

The sunk pool was surrounded by Ham Hill paving, ashlar retaining walls clothed with shrubs, and flights of steps, all constructed from the same iron-rich freestone, quarried and transported all the way from the West Country. The copings to the walls and plinths were all detailed with Classical mouldings, and with stone vases and sculpted balls arranged to emphasise the grandeur of the composition. It was theatrical in its conception and executed with two imposing semicircular stone seats placed at the end of twin axes on

top of the north side of the sunk lily pool. The seats were given prominence with busts raised on framing columns on either side. Their grandeur suggests they were intended to provide a vantage point from which spectators, looking over the sunk garden, could imagine themselves in the arena of the Coliseum and watch the games on the lawn, with the mansion as the stage back-drop. It was a brilliant conception with metaphor and analogy drawing on Peto's knowledge of Ancient Rome and the use of semicircular seats, which he had seen on the Street of Tombs at Pompeii.

The contemporary black-and-white photographs seen here capture the drama of the composition but not of course the colour. It is from the descriptions of the lily pool that we have to appreciate the horticultural delight of the arena. 'The lily canal', the *Gardener's Magazine* says, 'contains one of the finest collections of water lilies in the country …. Here, in addition to the finest of the forms in general cultivation, are splendidly developed specimens of such choice varieties as James Brydon, Robinsoni, Gladstoniana, and Willliam Doogue, which … yield freely of their floral wealth.' For those less familiar with these varieties this is nevertheless a spectacle of names to conjure with. The paved area was interrupted by borders and beds, and the planting was allowed to run freely to break up the rigid lines, although formality was retained by growing fine specimens of the upright glaucous Irish juniper at the corners of the beds and clipped Portugal laurels to give height and structure to the composition. Contemporaneous accounts describe how 'banks of Fuchsiae of mixed

varieties, with sprays of dark Heliotrope intermingling, make a fitting foil for the crimson flowers of the Penstemons'.

Still further away from the house beyond the Italian Garden and the formal elements of the ensemble – the *treillage* and the Ham Hill theatre – the different areas can be seen to fall into place as if this was a seventeenth-century landscape: the garden beginning with parterres in front of the house, followed by formal layouts in the middle, giving way finally to the *bosquet* or wilderness (those formalised wooded areas so much a feature of French gardens of that period). Here the composition was created with limes planted in lines to make alleys in quincunx formations. Overlooking this wilderness Peto designed and built a substantial tree house in the spreading crown of an ancient oak tree. The tree was in the centre of the eastern *bosquet* and commanded a view to the west down the main dividing alley.

The sketch for the design, which was called *Le Robinson*, shows an hexagonal structure with shingle walls, round windows, a walk-round balcony with balustrade, and columns supporting an overhanging thatched roof. In general outline the house was like the dairy at Easton, which was also thatched with spreading eaves. 'Le Robinson' was inspired by the area in Paris, known simply as 'Robinson', on the Rue de Malabry, where dozens of rustic restaurants were built on stilts and in trees in the late nineteenth century, reaching their heyday in the early 1900s. The first of the *bal-restaurants*, Le Grand Restaurant, had been opened in 1848 by an enterprising restaurateur capitalising on the vogue for tales of shipwrecks and the popularity of the novel about the Swiss Family Robinson who actually lived in a tree house. Peto's mischievous sense of humour would have enjoyed the allusion to the Robinsons, which in Paris offered all kinds of gastronomic delights, and no doubt much more entertainment for the less constrained.

Early photographs of the garden at Easton show standard limes, planted in lines, which were to be pleached later to form a box-edged hedge on clean stems. At that time looking over the clipped tops of the limes the tree house would have appeared like a cottage on a lawn, and it has been suggested that observation of the surrounding park from this elevated position served the same function as the Mount in Bacon's essay 'On Gardens' (1625). The tree house no doubt provided popular entertainment for the garden visitors. Daisy was fond of asking her friends to take tea with her in the 'crows nest'.

In 1907, there is mention of an American garden that had been recently formed to the east of the main formal areas. These gardens came into vogue around 1800 when 'American' gardens referred to the introduction of trees and plants from across the Atlantic,

Above: *Pitchford Hall, Shropshire: Peto would have been familiar with this well-known, rare survival of a reputedly early-eighteenth-century tree house. It is evidence of a long tradition of building rustic houses in trees and one that Lady Warwick was clearly keen to keep alive.*

Right above: *Elegantly hatted ladies lined up on the balcony of the grand tree house look down on the newly planted avenue of limes, which suggests that this photograph was taken soon after the garden was planted, c.1908.*

Right below: *Peto's sketch for a well-crafted tree house with balcony, which he titled 'Le Robinson'. He was referring to the area of Paris, Le Plessis Robinson, where tree-house restaurants had become fashionable in the nineteenth century following the excitement and fame of Swiss Family Robinson*

particularly the many conifers from the Pacific Coast. During Queen Victoria's reign, the use of the term was extended to refer to specialist areas set aside for the growing of acid-loving plants, which were then arriving from many regions of the world, especially China and Japan. At Easton, contemporary horticultural descriptions refer to the planting of 'large masses of heaths, azaleas, kalmias and other peat-loving plants.'

Returning to the north-west corner of the central garden, lawns and shrubs gave way to an open area between larger trees, with a path leading down a shallow vale, like the Grecian valley at Stowe – the Elysian fields, not this time leading to a Grecian temple, but bringing into view the first glimpse of the Japanese tea-house by the lake, partly dug or extended by the Salvation Army 'colonists'. Peto aptly described his sketch for the tea-house as 'Jap house in water', showing the wooden building and platform constructed on stilts so that it extended out into the lake. He roughly drew a wooden chinoiserie balustrade at the edge of an open verandah, with the enclosed tea-house behind. The platform with an open timber roof was clearly designed to carry wisteria from which blossoms would cascade down in the late spring, as he had so often seen in Japan. Fouquier in *De L'Art des Jardins* (1911) refers to the style as Chinese and the statues of Chinese women put there to give the illusion of reality. However, the house beside the verandah has a thatched roof more in common with the tree house and the dairy. Stone lanterns stand nearby which, together with the statues, were intended to provide the atmosphere of a Japanese garden, as indeed the planting does with bamboos, polygonums, Japanese iris and many other ornamental-leaved plants.

The garden at Easton more than any other of Peto's presented the widest range of experiences but the fortunes of Easton Lodge have not been good since Edwardian times, the house suffering another disastrous fire in 1918. The architect Philip Tilden describes visiting the house shortly after the fire and being told by Lord Warwick that it had been started by one of Daisy's pet monkeys. According to the story the monkey had wrapped itself in a blanket for warmth in front of the fire; the blanket had caught fire and then the monkey screaming and holding the flaming blanket aloft set light to the house in double quick time. Only part of the house was rebuilt. The garden fared no better. The pergolas collapsed under the weight of snow in the winter of 1922 (presumably the snow lying on the jute netting had been the cause); Lady Warwick died in 1938.

The American Air Force took over the house during the Second World War, the park was turned into an airfield and the garden slowly deteriorated through lack of maintenance. Much of the garden architecture was sold in the 1960s, and what was left fell into total decay and the land left in divided ownership, but recently, after some twenty years of work by the present owners to try and halt the decline, a Trust has been formed and complete restoration is its aim, although the expansion of the proposed runways at nearby Stansted Airport threatens the immediate environment of the garden and parkland.

WEST DEAN, SUSSEX

Peto's commission at West Dean could not have been more different from the ensemble of contrasting gardens at Easton Lodge. West Dean had one of the longest pergolas created in the Edwardian period, of even greater length than the two Easton pergolas put together; but although comparisons between them as regards scale are justified, there are no other similarities. The style and construction in each case was quite different: one was entirely made of wooden *treillage* with a curved roof, while the other was laid out with stone columns supporting horizontal beams. The two at Easton were key elements in a large overall scheme, while at West Dean the pergola never formed part of a comprehensive reworking of the Victorian garden. It traversed the slope commencing with the Jacobean garden house and finished on the edge of a sunk garden – arguably it started and ended

nowhere, disregarding Jekyll's advice that a pergola should 'always lead from one definite point to another'. The pergola at West Dean is essentially different; it is designed to stand alone and provides all the experiences of the pergola within its framework – it does not rely on integration with the garden that surrounds it.

The wealthy American William James, who had been at Harrow with Peto, bought the West Dean estate of 8,000 acres in 1891. The early meeting at school and the recognised success of Peto's architectural partnership with Ernest George, building large fashionable country houses and highly valued London town houses, was definitely a recommendation to James. He employed George and Peto to remodel and redecorate West Dean and install modern facilities to make it renowned as one of the most comfortable houses of the Edwardian period. Society came to stay at West Dean and included the Prince of Wales, who was an admirer of James's beautiful wife, and able hostess, the daughter of a Scottish baronet.

From the surviving records of the commission it is evident that Peto was very involved in the interior decoration of the house, writing to James in July 1892 about the silk panels for the dining room,

Left: *View from the pergola towards the garden house. The borders are crowded with herbaceous plants and the pergola is covered in climbers, but Peto's dictum that it should not be too dark has been adhered to. There is plenty of light striking through the rafters to illuminate the steps and the crazy- or 'map-paving', as he called it.*

Below: *The Classical columned pergola, leading to an undefined destination, breaks the golden rule: it begins and ends without much directional purpose. The traditional stone and flint garden house (seen here) makes a rather arbitrary starting point. However, whether it is the scale or the detailing, its stands admirably as a self-contained garden feature.*

describing the colour and the lighting and offering them to James at '£4 a piece', fifty-five being required. James accepted. Later in the same month Peto is discussing the hall panelling and suggesting that James should buy 'a very fine specimen of 16th century work', which would go very well with the period of the hall. Significantly, Peto's involvement in interior decoration continued in spite of his giving up the partnership with Ernest George in 1892, and in 1907 he gained the prestigious commission to design the interiors for the first-class accommodation on the Cunard 'flagship', *Mauretania*.

William James and Harold Peto must have remained good friends over the succeeding years, as proposals to construct a pergola do not seem to have been mooted before the summer of 1911. Also a further sign of their strengthened friendship is that while letters in the 1890s began with 'My Dear James', the first letter on 22 August 1911, discussing the pergola, is addressed to 'My Dear Willie'. From the contents it is clear that Peto had already made a visit to West Dean to talk over the garden house and pergola because he was now sending 'Willie' sketches for his consideration. Peto is persuasive about the *raison d'être* of the pergola, its length, its style and position. For him the starting point was the flint and stone garden house – traditional

Sussex materials which echoed the main house and the nearby flint walls – which he said 'would look charming under the big ilex'. One wonders if William James had called Peto to West Dean in the first place with the idea of asking him to build only a 'garden house', and that while they were on the lawn the idea of the pergola began to take shape. The planned structure, according to the letter, was to lead to the 'Rose Garden at the other end'. Apart from the beginning and the end, there is no suggestion that it should fit into any other scheme to develop the garden further.

The sketches, which have not survived, gave James alternatives for the style of the garden house 'one more classic in detail and the other more Tudor, I think the latter more in accord with the house perhaps. I think the chessboard of flint and stone would look *very* well and is a charming treatment of flint in Tudor Times.' Looking at the style and decoration of the garden house today one sees that Peto's suggestions must have met with favour: the walls are chequered, with knapped flint panels between ashlar Bath stone to form the 'chessboard', the

This panoramic view showing the bold scale of the pergola from garden house to pool still does not show all of it: a further section extends from the pool to the Rose Garden, away on the right. The 300-foot structure is the longest pergola to survive from the Edwardian era.

doorways with round Jacobean tops and the roof of cut stone domed in Tudor style. All, as Peto said, was very appropriate and in agreement with the style of the house.

In view of the length of the pergola, about 300-feet overall, Peto wrote about the importance of having a feature to engage the attention while walking from one end to the other. He proposed constructing a small tank that 'would make a delightful interlude either when walking along the pergola or looked at from the outside. We could put a little statue in tank as fountain.' This idea was accepted so that at the mid-point a tank occupies the entire width of the main path between the columns. On arriving at the tank, the path and pergola divide and run each side for two column lengths before uniting again to continue the walk. At this point, Peto gave the 'interlude' further emphasis by raising the roof with segmental arches, while leaving the space over the tank open to the sky. The prominence given to this central section recalls the domed *treillage* that was designed for Easton Lodge – both pergolas given a central climax between the two halves.

Peto suggested octagonal columns instead of circular ones in the first section after leaving the garden house – this he implied would be more in keeping with the Tudor style. However, in the built pergola all the columns are matching, round with Doric-style capitals, almost identical to the design he used for the single columns at Iford Manor, each with a hollowed abacus, presenting an overall appearance of simplicity, with the cross beams resting on wooden pads, and carved ends (*cyma recta* profile) that sit directly on top of the columns. The garden house stands slightly higher than the main length of the pergola so at the beginning the whole pergola is stepped down, with a ramped parapet to coincide with the steps.

Plans seem to have moved on quickly as they had already exchanged letters when Peto wrote again on 27 August giving further reasons for his preferred design. He expressly suggests not having a roof over the tank in order that the water lilies have enough light to encourage them to flower. He is most concerned about the appearance of the water in the tank: 'it is more for the *effect* of the water (I should line it with blue glass mosaic) and for the effect of a *break* in the roof, that I particularly want it.' His attitude to pergolas and light is heart-warming: 'I do not like pergola roofs to be a *dark tunnel* with branches crossing in a net work. You only get dead twigs inside where you walk and the birds flying overhead are the only people to enjoy the display of bloom. I like the rafters about 2 or 3 feet apart and the roses trained *along each* rafter, so you get a succession of garlands crossing over from side to side.' This letter gives us the best indication of what he wanted to achieve – not for him the dark tunnel arbours with not a rose to be seen.

His choice for the path material through the pergola was an interesting one, given that for the Italian Garden at Easton and the great terrace at Iford he spared no expense in obtaining dressed paving stones for large areas. He suggests in his letter to Willie that he should obtain prices for 'York stone map-paving', which we generally now call crazy-paving; the suggestion perhaps made on grounds of cost rather than Peto's preference, as he simply says, 'it looks very nice and cheaper than any other I think.' They seemed to have needed to confer on the exact position as he asks James to have the line of the pergola staked out in readiness for his next visit. However, some details of the pergola were still not agreed on by mid-September; Peto was concerned about the height of the columns and the appearance they would present over the full length. He was happy with some of them being 10-foot at the beginning, but over the longer length he was considering 9-foot 6 inches. These letters are a rare insight into his working methods, his attention to details and the need to assess them on the ground.

By early November, they had obviously reached agreement on the plans and cost, and Peto said he was charging a fixed sum of £100 for the work – from the few examples we have of fee scales he favoured a lump sum for the job rather than a percentage of costs. Some discussion takes place over the supply of roses. The 'Orléans' rose was, according to Peto's letter, much sought after and possibly available from a nursery in Lindfield, Sussex – this was a rose that Peto was very happy with at Iford ('it is a delightful rose, mine in full bloom *and* has been since *June*!' Note that he was then writing in November). By early December, the work was underway and Harris at the Westwood quarry, near Bradford-on-Avon, was beginning to send down by train the dressed stone to West Dean for work to start. By the end of December, the agent in charge at West Dean said that work was now well advanced and he was not keen to make any alterations to the design. However, not all went smoothly and there were still details unspecified; nevertheless work continued into the spring of 1912, and no doubt the intention was to have the pergola finished in time for spring planting.

The successful completion of the pergola was marred and possibly

Right: The columns of the pergola festooned with summer roses – the Edwardian rambler 'Debutante' and Clematis viticella 'Madame Julia Correvon'.

Below: The segmental arches with finials, seen here from the outside, give further emphasis to the point where the pergola divides to accommodate Peto's 'interlude' – the water tank.

delayed by the sudden death of William James in March 1912. The accounts, though, still testify to the completion of the work later that year; Mrs James would no doubt have seen that it was completed. Many years later, probably after the War, Edward James wrote to Peto enclosing a photograph of himself as a small boy laying the foundation stone on 5 January 1912.

The pergola stands today as an isolated and splendid structure spreading right across the sloping lawns to the north of the house. In recent years, there has been renovation to bring it back into a condition that very closely reflects Peto's vision of its light, open structure, planted up with roses and climbers surrounding the columns and tumbling from the roof beams. Along each side of the 'map-paving', Peto had planned borders between the central path and the foundation wall, which carried the columns – these are planted up largely with herbaceous plants, among them hostas and alchemillas to soften the path's edges. The pergola remains one of the longest to survive from the Edwardian era and shows Peto, although creating only a single feature in the garden, working with the generosity of scale that is one of the main characteristics of his work.

Top: *Peto's attention to detail is shown in the spacing of the cross beams to allow sufficient light for all the climbing plants.*

Above: *The form of the capital, Doric-style with hollowed abacus, is the same as that used for the single columns on the great terrace at Iford Manor and those of the casita portico at Ilnacullin.*

Left: *Given the length of the pergola, Peto divided the main axis approximately in the middle to surround a rectangular lily tank of two bays length. The tank was open to the sky, to encourage the water lilies to flower.*

CRICHEL HOUSE, DORSET

The vicissitudes of fashion in garden design are nowhere more evident than in the history of Crichel, although Peto's use of temples forms a useful link between the changes seen over the last two hundred years. The creation of great Italian terraces for Georgian country houses was very much the vogue in the 1840s, subscribed to, if not initiated, by the populariser of the Italian palazzo in England, the architect Charles Barry, and by the landscape gardener William Nesfield. Numerous are the examples, such as the terraces laid out at Holkham Hall and Harewood, where once eighteenth-century landscapes swept right up to the doors and windows of the house, creating for the English Palladians the natural balance between art and nature. The mid-Victorians turned away from this aesthetic ideal preferring to front the house with a level terrace of the utmost sophistication, in general with ornamental parterres and colourful bedding displays, from which to view the 'natural' parkland and the likely prospect of the lake. The new terrace at Crichel, although Edwardian, fulfilled this function absolutely.

The dwelling and the estates have passed down through the descendants of the same family for over three hundred years. Sir Nathaniel Napier built the first house in the early seventeenth century, and when his grandson, the second Sir Nathaniel, inherited in 1672, he converted and extended the Jacobean house into a more stylish post-Restoration house, laying out formal gardens in the fashion of the time. This house was burnt down in 1742, and following the rebuilding of Crichel in 1743 by Sir William Napier, the 4th Baronet, and the subsequent enlargement by his wealthy nephew in 1765, the new natural landscape setting for the house was then *à la mode*.

Above: *Views like this engraving of Crichel in its eighteenth-century park did not often survive the Victorian desire for terraces. At Crichel, change came with the more formal fashions of the Edwardian age. However, by the end of the twentieth century, the geometric parterre and the balustrades had gone, and the house now once again faces the parkland without formal intervention.*

Left: *The vast portico provides a wide-angled view over the staged parterre, which launches itself into the eighteenth-century landscape. The monumental colonnade frames an array of clipped topiary forms that stand in contrast to the floating branches of the distant parkland cedars.*

An eighteenth-century engraving published in Hutchins's *History of Dorset* (1774) shows the new house set in a picturesque landscape, with a grassy sward stretching down from the house to the lake to provide a perfect setting for the time. This landscape apparently survived the changing fashions of the nineteenth century until early in the twentieth century, when, as Avray Tipping writes, 'our own generation felt that a measure of formalism, by way of a neutral territory between the severe geometrical lines of the classic house and the free and waving lines of the contours, was desirable and called for.' Consequently in 1906, Harold Peto was brought in to lay out formal gardens once again, this time constructing a broad terrace, which projected out in front of the south portico, from which there were views over the park and down to the lake.

This level terrace with an open prospect to the south and east, and with the west embanked against gently rising ground, differs from Peto's usual style where he was more often seeking to plant in a way that focused attention on an inward-looking experience. There is no information as to how the commission progressed and the only inkling of his early thoughts for Crichel is in a small sketch on the house notepaper, which shows a long terrace extending from the house with six compartments, arranged symmetrically with three on either side of a central axis. More characteristic was Peto's apparent desire to enclose the garden with a tunnel arbour, a *berceau de verdure*, running down one side, an alley hedge on the other, and an arcaded semi-circular hornbeam hedge around the end. If this was the proposal for the garden then only the outline footprint was kept: the *berceau* to the west was replaced by a retaining wall on to rising ground, and the hornbeam hedge by a low balustrade forming a semicircular apron, which projected out into the park. In the far corners, on either side of the apron, were two small temples that provided perfect vantage points from which to take in the surrounding countryside. One can only surmise that when the commission was under discussion, the clients' abiding interest was to preserve the view of the park and lake from the grand portico – they were not interested in stepping down into an enclosed garden. Certainly contemporary photographs make much of the views that Peto's plan discloses, and it is only the temples that provide a little architectural transition from the terrace to that vision of tailored nature beyond.

The terrace was almost as broad as it was long, with the balustrade to the east and the retaining wall to the west being thrown out beyond the frontage of the house to allow steps on one side, and a walk on the other to be part of the great terrace platform. This apron was divided into four quarters (not six as in the preliminary sketch); each quarter formed of matching parterres which were slightly sunk below the two main dividing walks. Each axis was broad, the one centred on the portico, where it started, ran the length of the terrace to finish at the semicircular apron with wide views on all three sides. The cross axis was terminated at either end by Peto's favourite device, a semicircular stone seat which recalls those at Easton Lodge, Hartham and Iford.

From the piano nobile the immaculate carpet of colourful bedding has to be imagined against a formation of striking uprights. The rotunda, set in the distant corner of the parterre, with the park and the lake beyond are echoes of the eighteenth-century landscape.

The earliest *Country Life* photographs from 1908 show the garden in embryo with the shrubs only recently delivered from the nurseries and the beds still bare. What appears to be the temple already built in the corner of the garden was, in fact, according to the article, just a model constructed in this pre-eminent position to see whether the scale and proportions were totally satisfactory. Comparison with a later photograph of 1927 suggests that the model was deemed correct for its location, as the two temples look identical. The temple, like others that Peto was to design, was in the form of a rotunda, but differed in that it had a lead-roofed cupola, while generally, in others, open wrought-ironwork was used. That Peto liked these rotundas is evident from his sketches and from his collection of pictures and ephemera in which he included, among others, a view of the temple at Duncombe Park, Yorkshire – a rotunda of ten columns with Ionic capitals, which could have been the starting point for the design at Crichel. The scale and size have been adjusted for the site, but the Ionic capitals were selected as they matched the columns on the portico. The rotunda was eminently eighteenth-century in character to harmonise with the house and the surrounding parkland, and provided that invaluable link between the two.

The maturity of the planting on the parterre can be seen clearly in the photographs of 1925. The shrubs, mainly yews, now some twenty years old, were planted around the perimeters of the quarters next to the walks; they were arranged symmetrically to form pivotal obelisks at the corners, with intermediate truncated columns along each side. Within each sunk parterre there were standard mushroom Portugal laurels at every corner, and the parterre was laid out with simple panel beds, each quarter matching, and packed with what must have been huge displays of coloured bedding plants more typical of a High-Victorian garden than an Edwardian one. Gertrude Jekyll included the Crichel parterre in her second edition of *Garden Ornament* (1927). In a gesture to the seventeenth century the apron jutting into the parkland, beyond the quarters, was planted with the forms of a fleur-de-lys, symmetrically, on either side of the main axis. The whole carpet nature of the parterre was viewed either from the portico (on the *piano nobile*) of the house, or from the upper floors, and offered not the least obstruction to a clear view of the park and the distant gleam of water. Away from the parterre, a rectangular rose garden was designed *en treillage* with decorative arbours – Peto's *berceaux* in the style of the great French garden at Villandry. Later photographs show the whole structure festooned with roses.

The house was requisitioned during the War and the garden suffered accordingly – the balustrade, seats and temples were eventually sold off and the parterre garden grassed over. Once again in Crichel's history the great house stands marooned in the perfect setting of its eighteenth-century park, and the noble terrace on the south side has vanished.

Through the framing columns of the rotunda the house stands astride the parterre, overlooking the level plat from which the landscape can be enjoyed. In Avray Tipping's view, it formed a neutral territory between the Classical lines of the house and the natural contours of the park.

PETWOOD, LINCOLNSHIRE

At the beginning of his *Boke of Iford*, Harold Peto disapproves of the tendency for gardens to run riot, with 'masses of colour irrespective of form', and compares this with his experience in Japan reflecting that 'our English gardens must shock the austere taste of a Japanese whose art recognises the dominating need for form above everything.' Unlike Crichel with its sophisticated parterre, at Petwood simplicity of form was the keynote in the creation of the design. When he arrived, Peto found groves of young birch trees spreading over the level heathland and was inspired to use a broad structural form to match the wide horizons of Lincolnshire – a plan that showed a keen sense of place.

He began by laying out a simple axis that ran from a narrow terrace before the house to a distant temple as focal point. This was placed at the extreme limit of the overall designed area, the line only being interrupted by a raised terrace, which sat at right angles across the axis like a ship's bridge from which the captain overlooked the decks and the sea. Around this simple structure all Peto's favourite characters play their role: the pergola, the loggia, the sunk garden, the Alma-Tadema seats and the eye-catcher.

Grace Maple, the heiress to the famous London furniture store, chose to settle at the fashionable health resort of Woodhall Spa. She bought 40 acres of her favourite birch woodland on a sandy heath very close to the Spa early in the 1900s, and built an enormous house of numerous timber-framed gables, completed by 1905, which had the appearance of homely Port Sunlight, the picturesque village founded by William Hesketh Lever in 1888 to house his soap factory workers. In 1910, she married Captain Archibald Weigall, and Petwood, like

The temple rotunda (above) *was used as a focal point at the end of the long axis* (left) *leading from the house. Peto chose the strapwork stonework to complement the half-timbered, gabled mansion. But the cherubs on the Victorian urns are an anachronism, which he would never have recommended.*

West Dean and Easton Lodge, became famous for its lavish enter-tainment. The house surrounded by the sandy heath, not unlike the landscape that must have enclosed Jekyll's Munstead Wood, urgently needed a garden that would become the stage for the long hot summer and the Edwardian social calendar. Exactly how Harold Peto received the commission is unclear, but the plan that was acted upon is unmistakeably his work.

The *Country Life* writer Avray Tipping, who much admired this garden, described it as 'a broad vista studded with incidents', which is a useful description of the way variety and surprise have been woven into the garden tapestry. Leaving the house and descending the steps from the terrace, a broad flagged path led the eye to the most distant point: the Atalanta temple, which attracted the viewer like a magnet. The photographs down the main axis show a profusion of many varieties of roses growing on raised trellis and swags to either side of the path, which was bordered by the neatly clipped grey foliage of

lavender with flowering spikes. The raised terrace at the end of this path, in the centre of the layout, provided the interlude before proceeding to the destination: an opportunity to pause and turn aside, climb the steps and view the gardens from the 'bridge' and to take in the spread of the south front, described as 'a gabled villa of comfort but not of distinction'.

The garden could be viewed from above and traversed from east to west, and Peto's 'incidents' can be seen from a distance. The verna-cular-style house appears to have precluded the choice of a Classical balustrade for the terrace, so to be in keeping Peto settled for a Jacobean strapwork balustrade, not unlike the balustrade that

Above: *A broad, raised cross axis straddles the garden giving views in all directions over Peto's 'Jacobean' balustrade. A lone Pyghtle seat awaits the visitors, who could stroll across the terrace from end to end over the randomly coursed paving.*

Right: *The paving is lapped with a seemingly endless lavender hedge, and behind it a dense planting of rose bushes stands at the foot of espaliered climbers.*

surrounds the terrace of The Hall in Bradford-on-Avon. (As it is near to Iford, Peto would have known the house and a photograph of it appears in his archives). The broad flagged terrace, Jekyll said, had 'the exact degree of unevenness and patchwork that best suits a garden'. The paving stone joints give exactly that heightened sense of perspective that Peto was well aware of when he paved the great terrace at Iford. Gravel as a surface gives the eye a poor indication of perspective. Here at Petwood, the absence of people on the terrace walk seems at odds with a garden made for social occasions.

In spite of the attractions on either side, the distant eye-catcher over the second half of the garden beckons. The temple, like the ones at Crichel, was an open rotunda standing on a slight eminence with curving pergolas reaching out from either side. Tuscan columns and capitals (Ionic at Crichel) supported a simple entablature and then an open ironwork dome, surmounted by one of Peto's favourite statues: the fleet of foot Mercury, after the statue by Giambologna. What a

contrast this figure made to the lead figure of Atalanta below – hardly the athletic huntress she was assumed to be in the myth where she challenges her suitors to a race. This form of temple, and others like it, became generally known as 'Temples of Atalanta' in this period.

One of the most successful of Tipping's 'incidents' was the sunk garden in the lawn next to the pergola, which formed the western boundary of the site. The long rectangular pool at the centre, surrounded by paving and borders, with steps leading from each end and the middle of each side, is immediately comparable to Peto's design for the central Italian Garden at Ilnacullin – both have a central statue. In the case of Petwood, it was a sentimental pastiche of the celebrated fountain in the Palazzo Vecchio by Andrea del Verrochio, a *putto* with a dolphin, which spouted water above his head. A contemporary account described the pool with lilies and great clumps of Siberian iris in each of the four corners.

The focal point of the east side of the garden was the Classical loggia. This had none of the lightness and uplift of the pavilions at Hartham, Bridge House and Ilnacullin; it looked severe with its flat roof, four supporting Doric columns in stone and matching swagged urns on the roof. This edifice stood against a high brick wall, which stretched out making wings on either side, carrying niches for statuary, and was clothed with 'ivy, acanthus Veitchii, Gloire de Versailles and buddleias, jasmines and clematis.'

Confusingly, *Country Life* in 1915, described this eastern lawn as the Temple Garden and consequently the loggia as the temple. The writer said that just before War broke out the colour scheme for the garden was pink, mauve and purple, with 'great masses of delphiniums and phloxes in the beds'. Unlike other areas where paving flags were chosen, the apron in front of the loggia was made with irregular shaped stones – Peto's map-paving, which Jekyll referred to in *Garden Ornament* as 'crazy'. She asserted that there were circumstances where such paving was suitable – where stones

Above: *The sunk garden adds interest to the generally flat ground.*

Right: *The long rectangular pool, at its centre, is host to lilies and Siberian irises. It is formally planned, with steps descending symmetrically to the central paved area around the water.*

were naturally quarried like this – but she was more censorious about its use alongside Classical architecture. Peto would probably have agreed with her. However, the correspondence at West Dean indicates that in certain circumstances he was quite willing to save his clients expense and perhaps that was the case at Petwood.

Pergolas and many varieties of climbers were a dominant feature here. A lengthy pillar-and-beamed structure ran down the western boundary, another stretched out to either side of Atalanta's temple, and yet another one was erected over the sandy path leading to the Temple Garden. All exhibited a different style of treatment: the long one seen in the distance over the sunk garden has the appearance of a light wooden structure, the one next to the temple has wooden beams supported on stone Tuscan columns which match the rotunda, while the pergola in the Temple Garden has square, brick piers supporting wooden beams. This last pergola, the writer in his *Country Life* article tells us, terminated in a 'circular form', with at its centre 'a little stone figure playing with a bird.' The *putti* and related statues in this garden appear to be popular and rather sugary imitations of Classical originals. They look like 'off the shelf' examples and may well have been bought from firms such as John White's at the Pyghtle Works in Bedfordshire.

Against a vernacular background Peto avoided too many Classical references; the rotunda set beyond the pond is the one real exception, but standing as it did at the greatest distance from the house no conflict arises, and there, distant in the landscape, like the temple at Buscot, it alludes once again to the aesthetics of eighteenth-century Classicism. Avray Tipping is careful to draw attention to the open areas and groups of birches that were part of the 40 acres of heathland in which the garden was planned. This is the adroit Peto showing his sensitivity to the scope of the commission – there was no case for a parterre garden as at Crichel, or, as at Easton, mannered *treillage* pergolas around the croquet lawn. He relied instead on the axes to engender a sufficient degree of formality on which to hang, in a somewhat picturesque way, the arrival of 'incidents'– the bog garden, the simple pergolas, the natural lake, the rose garden and the sunk gardens – which interlock in a free form, not overloaded with geometric exactitude.

The *Country Life* article of 1915 ends with a poignant reminder of the times. In August 1914, guests were assembled at Petwood for the annual cricket festival when the outbreak of war was announced. Within twenty-four hours the guests had slipped away and Mrs Weigall had transformed the house into a military convalescent hospital, with resident medical staff and beds for some fifty soldiers. It is hard to imagine that the house and garden ever recovered the gaiety and carefree associations of the pre-war years. The garden has kept its bones but many of the 'incidents' have not survived.

Previous pages: Pergolas, loggia and terrace provide vertical emphasis to this predominately flat site. An abundance of roses has been used to clothe the bare masonry and timber. As elsewhere in the garden, sweet and un-Classical statues of cherubs have been used as focal points, which one assumes was the client's wish.

Right: The temple rotunda stands on the bank between the curved arms of a simple pergola, stretching out on either side. The elegant statue of Mercury crowning the temple is in contrast to the heavy figure of Atalanta below.

HIGH WALL, OXFORD

This was an entirely new development at Headington Hill on the outskirts of Oxford. The 20-acre site sloping to the west was acquired by an Edwardian lady, Miss Katherine Feilden, who employed the architect Walter Cave (1863–1939) to build a new house in a Tudor country-house style, from 1910–12. Walter Cave had trained under Sir Arthur Blomfield, and although he had a large urban practice, he was best known for his country houses. Lawrence Weaver, writing about High Wall in *Country Life* in 1917, said how rewarding it was to find a building on the outskirts of Oxford that was so successfully in line with the city's Tudor traditions. Cave chose to place the house at the extreme north-east end of the site, close to Pullen's Lane, with the principal elevations to the south and west. Although the land fell away to the west to give fine views over Oxford's spires and towers, to the south it rose to block out the distant landscape. Thus, when Harold Peto was called in to design the garden he was confronted with an unpromising location.

In front of the western façade, Peto was able to make good use of the falling ground with a series of terraces and steps to capitalise on the views, but planning the garden to the south to provide an interesting outlook from the house was harder. More difficult still was to design it so that both parts of the garden flowed easily together. The south front had been planned symmetrically, with an arcaded loggia at its centre and projecting bays at each end. It seems more than a coincidence that the simple appearance of the loggia at High Wall was like the one Peto had built at Iford Manor; perhaps there had been some degree of cooperation between Cave and Peto, because both planning and construction of the garden were well under way by 1912 when the house was finished.

From the loggia a stepped apron led down to a broad flagged path, which surrounded the house on two sides. Beyond the path and lawn to the south, Peto must have built the high brick retaining wall to the east, which by necessity ran diagonally across the garden and then turned through nearly 90 degrees to cross the southern view. He was therefore faced with an unfavourable triangular piece of ground into which to fit a garden.

The key feature he designed was an articulated pergola, which provided a shady walk around the central lawn, but chiefly it skilfully concealed the awkward angle and height of the wall. Given these constraints the central lawn was placed across the east-west axis; half the lawn therefore was opposite the south front and the other half joined the western terraces, thus uniting the two gardens. As the photograph taken from inside the house loggia shows (see page 68), the central arch frames the flagged path to the entrance of the pergola. A bank of lavender to the left stretches along the path against a low

A symmetrically planned house was sited opposite the high wall, which cut the space obliquely. Peto's balanced 'U'-shaped pergola lines up one of its arms with the loggia and the other with the terrace walk. The wellhead is placed at the centre between the two axes.

parapet wall and defines the boundary of this side of the lawn. It is matched by a boundary wall on the far side, which forms the parapet wall of the main west-facing terrace.

The pergola, which stands up against the high wall and surrounds the end of the lawn on three sides, differs from Peto's other pergolas in England, but was reminiscent of the wide use of pergolas in the Riviera gardens of the time. (In particular, the curving structure at Isola Bella near Cannes makes an interesting comparison). Through the arch on the right in the same photograph, the open-fronted garden house can be seen forming the central feature of the curving pergola, directly on the axis which splits the lawn, and runs along the west front. The garden house is a medley of stylistic details, quite unlike the elegant pavilions Peto designed for Hartham and elsewhere, and has Classical Tuscan columns supporting a tiled and faceted vernacular roof, similar to the roof on the garden house at Iford. Throughout the pergola he used Tuscan columns, echoing those of the loggia, with carved pads on top to support the running beams, which in turn supported the cross beams – a pergola construction similar to that at West Dean, where Peto was working at practically the same time. However, at High Wall Peto sat the columns on a raised brick parapet, with stone copings to give a clear boundary to the edges of the lawn. The planting, at least in the photographs of 1917, shows an absence of roses in favour of deciduous climbers, such as wisteria and *Vitis coignetiæ*, while herbaceous plants tumble out of the space at the foot of the walls.

The western terraces were the perfect complement to the view. This elevation, like the one on the south front, is also perfectly balanced with three bays: the two larger outside ones being made of brick with stone surrounds to the windows, while the central bay is

Above: The high terrace, with Peto's favourite balustrade, runs across the garden to the pergola, and is cut at right angles by the east-west axis. It crosses the south elevation, and a wide flight of steps descends to the lower garden.

Right: The house seen from the south west. The pergola, which began opposite the central loggia, opens out on the top terrace in line with the paved way that runs across the west elevation. The lower terrace, with espaliers trained along the retaining wall and a hedge on the other side, makes a long grassy bowling alley.

smaller, recessed and of ashlar masonry. The main terrace wall has a central projection that duplicates the bay of the house, and a stone balustrade with mid-waisted balusters following the style of the balusters on the gabled parapet walls on the south side. This again suggests possible cooperation with Walter Cave as it is the same design as Peto used for the lily-pool balustrade at Easton Lodge. The retaining walls of the terraces, in keeping with the house, are brick. The key central path descends to the lower garden with a series of stone steps and terraces, crossing a bowling alley that straddled the garden, with a retaining wall along which fruit trees were espaliered. The flights of steps continued, framed with topiary and borders with a rose garden below.

Lawrence Weaver in *Country Life* alludes to the contemporary fashion for using 'old figures in new gardens'– a fashion which Peto apparently followed. However, the article continues by quoting from Vernon Lee's essay 'About Leisure' (1897), in which she is disparaging about such fashions. (Vernon Lee and Peto had met in Florence but there is no information about what they thought of each other.) Although there was a profusion of statuary at Petwood, mainly of the new kind based loosely on Classical originals, there was notably none to be seen at High Wall, and Weaver concludes: 'Today their employment has become so usual that the absence of a host of lead *amorini* at High Wall strike the eye almost as a novelty and as something of a relief.'

This view from the central loggia keys in with one arm of the pergola, as the high retaining wall to Pullen's Lane has forced the garden house off centre.

2:
Canals,
Pavilions
and
Bridges

Wayford Manor, Somerset: (above) *Peto's loggia on the terrace.*
Bridge House, Surrey: (left) *The well-planted terrace beside the summerhouse.*

I
T IS immediately apparent in an overview of Peto's work that for him water was a vital element in a garden ensemble. So, it is surprising that he writes very little about its use in *The Boke of Iford* and makes only the occasional reference to it in his diaries. Brief though these mentions are they are nevertheless indicative of how he considered water could fulfil an aesthetic role in the landscape; and as always he was acutely aware of its historical context. In *The Boke*, as might be expected, he recalls the part played by water in old Italian gardens, where among other features he refers to the 'picture being painted with Cypress hedges, canals and water-tanks'. His formal use of water derived from Italy, France and the Moorish gardens of Spain, while his enthusiasm for the Robinsonian natural approach came from his trip to the East.

When at Hori-Kiri in Japan, 'this Mecca' for iris plants, he is full of joy at describing the scene and notes the iris tanks and open sheds from which to "view" the flowers'. At Kyoto, he revels in the reflections of the spring blossom, while at Nikko he delights in gardens where 'gushing little waterfalls coming tumbling into them from the

hills and thence in little streams running hither and thither in every direction among the stones with little swampy side bits occasionally full of iris – they are a lesson of gardening possibilities.' (Those 'possibilities' had to wait until he made his own garden at Iford Manor). On another note, he relates how he feels pure enjoyment feeding the goldfish at Miyanoshita where the 'effect was most beautiful as the whole shoal of every conceivable tint, grey, black, gold, white, scarlet and piebald all rush together and struggle so that some are forced quite out of the water on the backs of others'.

Unexpectedly, in spite of his fascination with water, ostentatious fountains play little or no part in his gardens; his ideal was to have a small fountain playing gently in a pool where just the murmur of water could be heard. His view of formal water gardens also encompassed lily pools and canals, using the surface of the water to be the mirror of all that surrounds it – for this effect water movement caused

by large fountains would be disruptive. 'Water', said the French seventeenth-century writer Jacques Boyceau, 'is necessary to a garden for its irrigation and refreshment during drought, but it also serves to embellish, especially running water in streams. Its vivacity and movement are the living spirit of the garden.' Harold Peto would have been in full agreement.

The large sculptural fountains of the Victorian period, fountains like those that William Nesfield created for Witley Court, Worcestershire, were generally seen as quite *outré* and ill-suited to the old style English garden. In William Robinson's *English Flower Garden* (1883) the short section on fountains is cautionary: 'In this moist climate of ours water needs to be used with great discretion', and continues to argue that monumental fountains have little place in England. Thomas Mawson and Gertrude Jekyll both emphasised the important part that water plays in the garden, but the examples they cite were mainly pools and the use of fountains was very restrained.

Undoubtedly, Peto's water features were among the most ambitious of the Edwardian era. At Easton Lodge, the lily pool in the Italian Garden was one of the grandest schemes of its kind, orchestrated with a surrounding balustrade that could match the finest Italian *nymphaea* at the Bobili Gardens, Celsa, and others. The single vista of descending rills and pools at Buscot Park is unmatched for scale and conception by any comparable examples in England. Hartham Park and Bridge House both present jewel-like Dutch-style arrangements, with canals in front of pavilions, which although Italian in form, are reminiscent of the composition of the canal and garden house at Westbury Court, Gloucestershire. The streamside landing stage at Heale House is unique and once appreciated utterly unforgettable. At Petwood and Ilnacullin, the pool in the sunk garden surrounded by its steps and borders gives a touch of otherness – as the *Country Life* writer said of Petwood in 1915, ' it conveys an indefinable sense of calm seclusion and studied aloofness'.

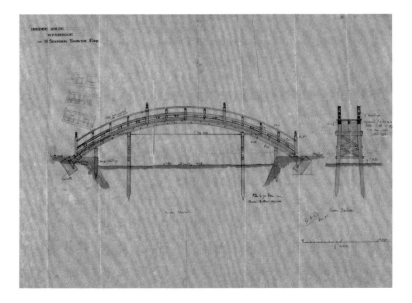

Top: *At Hartham Park, Wiltshire, the pavilion overlooks the lily pool and the bridge spanning the long canal.*

Sumiyoshi Bridge, Osaka, Japan: (centre) *When Peto visited Japan in 1898, he travelled widely and took note of many features, although he made no particular mention of this bridge. However, it bears a striking resemblance to the sketch, dated 1905, for Bridge House, Surrey (below).*

BUSCOT PARK, OXFORDSHIRE

During a ten-year period Harold Peto carried out at least two important commissions for Lord Faringdon at Buscot: the first creating a new entrance approach and the second the Water Garden for which Buscot is justifiably renowned. Buscot Park is a grand eighteenth-century house standing on raised ground in what remains of its early parkland, with views in all directions. The Loveden family built the main house and lived at Buscot until they sold the estate to an Australian tycoon, Robert Campbell, in 1859. The sale particulars described the property as 'a noble mansion with finely-timbered parks and pleasure grounds, two large ornamental lakes, beautiful woodlands, plantations and covers', a domain of 3,558 acres. The new owner, having made his wealth from gold trading in Australia, invested heavily in his new estate, but his enterprising attempt to make a business of distilling spirits from sugar beet failed, and two years after his death the estate was again sold in 1887 to Alexander Henderson (later 1st Lord Faringdon).

Robert Campbell had made significant changes to the estate during his tenure, which provided the foundations on which Peto began his work in 1904. The large lake lying a quarter of a mile to the east of the house had been created before 1800 in the late phase of the parkland development, and the conveyance plan of 1860 shows a carriage drive passing to the north east between house and lake. But by 1876, Campbell had begun the transformation of the pleasure grounds, replacing the carriage drive to the north east with an arboretum walk down to the boat house; it was the first section of this walk, showing up as a straight axis on the early maps, which was later to form the first part of Peto's Water Garden.

Alexander Henderson (1850–1934) had been a successful city financier and no doubt his zealous promotion of railway companies put him in touch with Harold Peto's father, Sir Morton. After his acquisition of the Buscot estate the thriving partnership of George and Peto was, therefore, the obvious choice for any planned structural refurbishment of the house, which took place around 1890. It followed that when Peto left the partnership in 1892 to concentrate on landscape design, he was chosen to undertake the garden commission. Between 1904 and 1913, he was principally involved at various stages in creating the axial Water Garden from the house to the lake, and the addition of a new forecourt on the south entrance front. The style of two bridges on the estate indicates that he had a hand in their design, too.

When Peto was contracted in 1904, his brief was to design the first section of the Water Garden commencing about halfway down the existing but now overgrown long axis, starting with the first and most

A dramatic entrance to the Water Garden down a long flight of steps between two ancient river gods, which Peto is thought to have found in Naples. Note the use of 'map-paving' (which he had also recommended for West Dean) between the parapet walls, while the path beyond has regular coursed paving.

ornamental of the pools which was quatrefoil in shape. It was centred on a copy of a Classical Roman fountain, here made in bronze but based on the marble original in the Naples Museum, of the winged *amorino* tumbling upside down in the coils of a dolphin's tail. The view from here down the long canal to the distant temple, framed by the water spouts from either side of the dolphin's head, is one of the finest water garden vistas of the twentieth century.

To accentuate this fantastic pool that marks the beginning of the Water Garden, Peto placed large semicircular, Roman-style stone seats against the hedge on either side. The seats with carved lion's head ends are of the same design he used for the single seat on the alley at Easton Lodge. The water flows out of the quatrefoil basin down a narrow rill before spreading out into a long rectangular tank, with the border hedges thrown back to make a long, wide enclosure, open at the far end where the water leaves the pool under a small bridge and then continues on its journey to the lake. This first phase of the construction of the Water Garden ended at this point with a bridge that carried a path from the south bank over the canal to reach the boathouse to the north.

The bridge, too heavy for some, is reminiscent of those in Peto's favourite city, Venice. It is small in scale crossing only a narrow rill with a low eighteenth-century-style balustrade matching the one that surrounded the forecourt. At Hartham Park, a bridge of similar style and scale crossed the canal in front of the pavilion. Stone balls on the balustrade of both give these miniaturised bridges a touch of elegance. The paving flag edgings accentuate the striking line of the stone-walled canal from the quatrefoil fountain basin to the bridge that terminated this phase of the work – the rill in this section had a number of cascades and the paving edge was stepped accordingly. The water level in Peto's drawings indicates that he planned for it to be within a few inches of the ground level – a principle emphasised by Gertrude Jekyll in *Gardens for Small Country Houses* (1912), 'the water should be kept at its proper level, which is as high as is possible. The nearer it is to the kerb of the pool, the wider and more beautiful will be the reflections.' Current water levels at Buscot are far below the pool edge.

Peto was called back seven years later to undertake further work. One can only speculate whether he had thought he would complete the project when the work was originally commissioned, or perhaps it was postponed for practical reasons. But, it is hard to believe that when Peto conceived the idea for the project he did not have a vision of a completed walk from house to lake. His opportunity came in 1912, when it was reported in the *Architectural Review* that 'Mr Peto's suggestion to carry on the scheme to the lake at its lower level with a long *pièces d'eaux'* was agreed to, as well as the design, at the top, of the flights of steps up to the house.

The fall from the little bridge to the lake is slight and after a further section of rill the waterway widens again, this time to form a very narrow elongated tank with a large round pool at its centre, thus

An overview of the watercourse from the stairway to the distant temple, completed in at least two phases from 1904 to 1912. This foreshortened view unifies the different elements of the composition.

recapitulating the sequence of geometric shapes – round, quatrefoil then rectangular, and finally rectangular and round to finish. The flagged paving that forms the edge and delineates the canal also outlines the semicircular halves of the central pool. The hedges that enclose the water alley follow the simple contours of the watercourse. From here the canal flows out into the lake, and the temple stands as the unreachable goal on the other side of the water.

The transition from the house to the long canal was the next essential step in setting up the vista and concealing the oblique angle between axis and house – without close scrutiny the assumption is easily made that the long axis of the house and that of the alley are the same. Taking the route east from the north Victorian-Italian terrace through a grove of trees, the new stairway is framed at the top by two river gods carved into the form of Cipollino marble columns (one of Peto's acquisitions made in Naples), with the view down the alley clear all the way to the lake. The plan of the steps, dated January 1912, echoes the form of the newly constructed basin in the last section of the watercourse, having a circular section in the middle, with curved seats on either side, and a central 'fountain or sundial' and four cypresses. The elevation of the new stairway shows a low 'ramped' parapet wall of rag stone and ashlar quoins, and coping with breaks marked by oil jars, these last not incorporated in the completed design. There had been some existing piers in this part of the alley and Peto suggested making arches over the steps rather like a Renaissance arbour – this was not carried out. The floor panels

Above: *The balustraded bridge provides a real and aesthetic crossing point. Its miniaturised scale perfectly complements the rill and its chain of pools.*

Left: *The round basin at the end of the water alley is now the foreground for a view back to the stairway approach. Old oil jars placed on the margins give another clue to the analogy with a Roman garden.*

between each flight of steps were finished with his 'map-paving' as was used at West Dean – often preferred by Peto when the path was contained by low parapet walls.

The river gods, now moved to another location by the lake, once stood in their pre-eminent position as guardians of the walk; their presence evoking the spirit of the waterway and a metaphor for the river. Peto was metaphorically referring us back to Roman life where the gods were necessary and powerful as guardians of the house as well as the garden. In Pompeii, the Egyptian god of the Nile, Osiris, was often depicted, but in the garden of the House of Loreius Tiburtinus, the Nile itself was symbolically represented by water cascading down from the terrace intð a long canal, which ran the length of the garden, interrupted by fountain basins and a temple. Statuettes and herms were placed in the greenery along its margins. This could be a description of the alley at Buscot with all its Classical

references and the semicircular seat, another version of the one that stands outside the Gate of Herculaneum on the Street of the Tombs.

While Peto was working on the extension to the watercourse he was also designing a new approach to the entrance front of the house. He remodelled the forecourt enclosing it with balustraded walls, chained bollards and stone gate piers. Since then a further re-planning and enlargement was undertaken in the 1930s, which resulted in Peto's gate piers being moved to the position they are now in, on a realigned south-east approach, which can be seen in the photograph shown above.

Essentially the chain of water features and canals, extending from the house to the lake, are today as Peto planned them with the exception that some of the statuary and the oil jars have been moved. The Long Alley is still enclosed by formal clipped hedges, which frame the view and concentrate attention during the measured progress towards the distant prospect. It is a fine example of a garden created entirely without the embellishment of flowers, to which a contemporary writer in 1913 added, 'the whole effect is one of extraordinary peace and dignity'. This is still undeniably the case today.

HARTHAM PARK, WILTSHIRE

A landscape designer rarely has the kind of opportunity that was presented to Harold Peto when he took up the commissions for Easton Lodge and Ilnacullin. Buscot had given him another golden opportunity – he was able to plan a linear feature in its entirety almost in isolation from neighbouring views. He was effectively presented with a corridor leading to the lake, which he could make his own creation unconnected to an existing scheme. In contrast at Hartham, although there is no first hand information on the architect's brief, he was asked to add an appropriate culmination to the long terrace, and within the walled kitchen garden to create a pleasure garden that by necessity had to be self-contained. Very different aspects of Peto's work were called upon – one relatively simple, while the other gave him the chance of reworking a cherished ideal with canal and pavilion. However, he had to work within these constraints and there was apparently never the choice of re-planning the landscape around the house.

Sir John Dickson-Poynder, who employed Peto, was born with a silver spoon in his mouth. He succeeded to the baronetcy in 1884 at

the young age of eighteen, and then only four years later inherited Hartham Park along with a considerable fortune. By 1892, he was already MP for Chippenham, which is close by. Early on he must have consulted Harold Peto about new gardens for Hartham, but probably not before Peto had become a relatively near neighbour at Iford Manor in 1899. Major work in the garden was completed by 1907, when photographs of it showing a few years of maturity appeared in *The Studio*'s publication *The Gardens of England*, so it can be assumed that Peto was planning the garden around 1903 – much at the same time as he was working at Easton Lodge. How much Sir John saw of his garden is debatable as he was initially at work in London as a successful politician, then later served as Governor-General of New

Above: *A Victorian terrace laid out immaculately on the garden front, with geometric beds planted with colourful half-hardy annuals of the day. A balustrade demarcates the entire area, but there is nothing particularly to identify any signs of a new design. Peto conceivably may have contributed some accents to the stonework.*

Right: *The newly planted area within the old kitchen garden walls can be seen through the columns of one of Peto's Classic pavilions, similar to those at Ilnacullin and Villa Maryland. He took the opportunity to design a small bridge over the canal which, although much simpler, can be compared in scale to the one at Buscot.*

Zealand from 1910 to 1912 and made Lord Islington; all this must have kept him from home. However, in those social Edwardian times there are records of Asquith, Churchill and Prince Arthur, the third son of Queen Victoria, staying at the house, so presumably this was one reason why new gardens were required.

James Wyatt had built the present mansion in 1790–95, but it was much added to during the nineteenth century and in particular after Sir John had inherited. The photographs show that the south front looked over a large expanse of lawn set out in typically Victorian mode, with large island beds packed with bedding annuals across the centre and clipped shrubs arranged symmetrically around the perimeter. The lawns were surrounded with wide gravel paths, and the entire terrace was enclosed with an unremarkable balustrade and all on the same level as the surrounding park. It seems unlikely that Peto would have had a hand in any of this.

To the west, lay a long raised walk projecting south and fitting rather uncomfortably on the side of the house. As a gesture to unite them, a copy of the Warwick Vase (by hearsay carved from a single block of Bath stone quarried from the excavations in the construction of nearby Box tunnel) was placed to provide a focal point, viewed from the south terrace, and at the same time to mark the commencement of the raised walk. The Warwick Vase, in its turn, was a copy of the famous Greek urn that had been brought back to this country in pieces during the eighteenth century and finally restored at Warwick Castle. If the story of the origin of Hartham's copy is true then clearly Peto had no hand in its design, but conceivably he had it placed there to emphasise the beginning of the walk.

The *Country Life* article of 1909 refers specifically to the design of this raised terrace, with the path running between 'immense herbaceous borders' to arrive at the south end where Peto planned a small balustraded area, with a semicircular seat to terminate the vista. The balustrade matched the one enclosing the south lawn, and the carvings on the ends of the Roman seat were of the same pattern as that used at Hinton Admiral, the two seats overlooking the pool arena at Easton and the one at Bridge House – all five seats were closely copied from the example at Pompeii, which was used for the painting *An Exedra* by the Victorian artist Alma-Tadema.

At the entrance to the enclosed area Peto placed a pair of white marble urns from Verona, decoratively carved and finished with a sprig of leafy ironwork emerging from the top. From this enclosure a small gateway led out to the west into an open area with small trees and shrubs leading to the circular Rose Garden, which at its centre had a winged lion on a column – a replica of the original standing in the Piazzetta in Venice. Peto could have/supplied this as he did perhaps the one for Lady Warwick's garden at Easton. The Rose Garden surrounded by its yew hedge was part of a circuitous route leading to the walled kitchen garden that was to be transformed from its utilitarian mode into a secluded pleasance.

The Water Garden, for that is what it became, was probably hot on

The design of the quadrant arms of the pergola, which embrace the pool on either side of the pavilion, is very similar to those at Bridge House. The paved way over the bridge leads directly to a small Classical loggia against the wall of the former kitchen garden.

the heels of the one at Easton or possibly its twin. The treatment though, of necessity, had to be inward-looking and to be discovered within the walls like a pearl in its shell – it was to become a garden of contemplation with none of the spectacle of the arena at Easton. In scale, and in William Morris's words, 'well fenced from the outside world', it shares more in common with Bridge House, another water garden in which to walk and meditate on the central theme. A broad canal was built right across the centre of the garden on a north-south axis which split the area into two halves; at the head of the canal against the south-facing wall, Peto built one of his iconic summer houses or, as Jekyll sometimes called them, garden pavilions. The pavilion was one of three Peto built in England and Ireland, the other two being at Bridge House and Ilnacullin. The architectural detailing of the fronts of all three derives from the Italian Renaissance – all three are designed with three bays divided by Classical Ionic columns – but after that the permutations in the individual designs are varied.

At Hartham and Ilnacullin there is a single raised arch in the centre of the pavilions, but the roof-lines are quite different; Hartham has a steep-pitched stone-tiled roof and finials in keeping with the vernacular houses of the surrounding neighbourhood, while Ilnacullin has a shallow-pitched slated roof which, among other connotations, echoes

the line of the distant Irish hills. The pavilion at Bridge House has three equal arches like the loggia at Iford Manor, but the pitch of its pantiled roof is shallow. The pavilions at Hartham and Bridge House stood at the head of T-shaped canals and carried pergolas to either side, while at Ilnacullin the pavilion is the focal point across the sunk garden, and of the three it is the only one that has the same elevation front and back and through which you can walk. The façade of Hartham's pavilion, with a raised central arch, has often been compared with that of the Loggia of the Muses at the Villa Lante, Bagnaia, as a possible source of inspiration.

The 'Dutch garden' at Westbury Court featured in *Country Life* would have been well known to Peto, whose great friend Avray Tipping lived at nearby Chepstow. This could have been the inspiration for both the canal gardens at Hartham and Bridge House. Westbury has a T-shaped canal and another long canal with the Dutch pavilion at its head. The similarities are obvious, but Peto, rather than choosing to enclose the canals with hedges, preferred to leave the

Above: *The prominent kerbstone, which surrounds the long canal, suggests that Peto may have been planning a balustrade, rather like the one at Easton Lodge, but if so that part of the scheme was abandoned. The pavilion across the head of the canal invites an immediate comparison with Bridge House.*

Right: *A modern lead figure, not to Peto's taste, holds up a sundial to passers-by.*

space open on either side to draw maximum reflection from the sky. Hartham had its own specific architectural details: the canal was rounded at the south end, like the ends of the pool at Easton, and was surrounded by a stone kerb – this seems at variance with the desire to have the water accessible and approachable as at Bridge House and Buscot. Speculation suggests that Sir John was originally thinking of having an entirely balustraded pool like the one at Easton, hence the kerb, which would have carried the balustrade. To support this theory is the presence, at the head of the canal opposite the pavilion, of a balustrade that could have been continued.

Another striking feature was the small low bridge, crossing the canal just opposite the pavilion. Arguably it cut off the view but alternatively its small scale, like the one at Buscot, provided a dynamic adjunct to the canal and also to the imposing structure behind. Its curved form and arching balustrade had a close parallel to the Japanese Nikko Bridge, which Peto had seen only a few years before in 1898. The Hartham bridge, like the one at Buscot which carried the path to the boathouse, also had a practical function: the eastern entrance to the walled garden is on the axis that runs in front of the pavilion, carrying the path to the small Classical-style loggia against the western wall.

From the photographs it is clear that flagstone paving was used throughout; this was Peto's preference for all his edgings for canals, as at Buscot and Bridge House and the surroundings to the pool at Easton. A certain profusion of plants can be seen growing freely round the canal sides between the kerbstone and the paving. Judging by photographs of Iford at this period, Peto would have encouraged such random and serendipitous growth, but this was not to the liking of the garden writer A. L. Baldry in his article 'The Gardens of England': 'A touch of the same deliberate carelessness can be seen in the garden at Hartham Park where the severe lines of the architectural laying-out … have been softened by … the accidental growth of vegetation in unexpected places … it gives, perhaps, a hint of neglect which has produced effects not really allowable in formal gardening.' Peto would have thoroughly disagreed, as indeed would have Jekyll.

The planting down the borders of the canal appears to be irises fringed with lavender – a favourite choice. The growth of the climbers on the pergolas to either side of the pavilion seems to have been well advanced by the time the photographs were taken in 1909. Ornamental vines are also well spread out on the balustrade that runs along the front of the pool. Pyramid bays can be seen in tubs on either side of the pavilion to soften the edges where architecture meets vegetation. Mature lollipop trees stand beside the bridge, and the old espalier apples in the distance have been kept to denote the lines of the old kitchen garden paths.

Today, the garden is in private hands, but not all Peto's garden features have been preserved: the Long Walk and the semicircular seat are still *in situ* but the canal has gone, although the isolated garden pavilion still stands proudly where it was built.

A copy of the famous Warwick Vase, made before Peto's time, was probably placed by him on the raised terrace walk overlooking the Victorian plat and the parkland beyond.

BRIDGE HOUSE, SURREY

The similarities between Bridge House and Hartham Park are immediately obvious – a T-shaped canal with a serene pavilion at its head and elsewhere in the garden an 'Alma-Tadema' Roman seat – but the differences are far from apparent. At Bridge House, the whole garden was planned as a cohesive series of very different experiences. In this respect, it has something in common with Petwood, as the *Country Life* description in 1908 makes clear: 'Not a comprehensive design of which the parts are subordinated and disciplined to the rule of the central idea, but a set of little horticultural communities preserving much individual independence and only loosely knit together into a whole … *multum in parvo.*' However, at Bridge House the Water Garden and other incidents were much more than a community of plants.

As is the case with so many of Peto's gardens, there is a lack of information that tells us anything of the history of the site or the commission at Bridge House. Records of the house suggest that it was built in the 1840s, a modest affair with bays and Georgian windows, stucco walls – not typical of fashionable Victorian houses of this period. It was called Grove House then and changed its name to Bridge House in 1890, when Henry Seymour Trower bought it. He was described as a connoisseur of art and a great collector of Japanese art, and when he died in 1912 a catalogue of his important collection was published. As well as having Bridge House, Trower continued living in London, in Bryanston Square, where he moved in the literary and artistic circles of the time, which included such luminaries as Whistler, Beerbohm, Berenson and James. He was born in 1843 and in 1871 married Juliet Salomons who, according to the author of the article on Bridge House in the *Gardeners' Chronicle* in 1903, had by then taken the garden in hand. Avray Tipping, in a later article of 1908, draws attention to the time the house was purchased in 1890 when the landscape 'wholly lacked character and interest' – a lawn stretched down to the river and the rest of the ground was field; the only attractive feature was the mature trees, many of which were kept. The first phase of the garden's development was completed during the 1890s, and some of it appears to reflect the wishes of Mrs Trower rather than Peto's more formal style. She is described in the 1903 article as encouraging the natural style of the garden, augmenting the existing trees with all the available plants and shrubs to contribute to 'the artistic and natural beauty of the whole'. However, it is also clear from the description that Peto, although not mentioned by name, was already at work there. This comes as no surprise as according to Peto's visitors' book, which was started in 1893 when he moved from London to Kent, the Trowers were regular guests.

The *Gardeners' Chronicle* refers to a secluded garden just to the north of the house enclosed with what it calls an 'elaborately worked

When Peto became friends with the Seymour Trowers, who bought the house at Weybridge in the 1890s, he designed this captivating open-air summerhouse to adjoin the south-west corner.

Above: *This enigmatic scene of a mysterious lady in white sitting beside the temple,
down the path from the Belvedere Apollo, has all the constituents to make a story.*

Left: *This small enclosed garden at the side of the house, with its curved Roman seat
(just visible at the right of the photograph) and ornate seventeenth-century-style* treillage *screen
beyond the small lily tank, is very much Peto's vision.*

wooden screen'. This was probably Peto's first use of seventeenth- and eighteenth-century *treillage,* developed from his drawings of Blondel and others, which was to flower later in the enormous pergolas he designed at Easton Lodge. At Bridge House, this small example has just a touch of finesse, with its fluted pilasters, Ionic capitals and pineapple finial – all drawn in a small sketch, which survives at Dumbarton Oaks, in Washington. The screen in this position, standing without apparent connection to other episodes in the garden, looks for all the world as if it were there to conceal what lay beyond – this is where the kitchen garden was located – and not included as an adjunct to the formal garden. But, no doubt it had also been borne in mind that the neighbour's boundary was close, and local records show that Weybridge at that time was up for development to house the affluent overspill from London. It was described as 'a successful suburb' where 'new houses crop up almost like mushrooms'.

A Roman seat can be seen on the right of the *Country Life* photograph, with ends of the same design as those used at Hartham and other Peto gardens. But, it differs in one significant respect: the seat was inscribed on the back with words from the opening line of Robert Herrick's poem *To Virgins, to make much of time*: 'Gather ye Rose-buds while ye may'; it seems ironically appropriate for a seat for which the original version served as a constant reminder of life's passing. There are other associations that can be made between the lines of the poem and the garden features at Bridge House, such as the rising and setting sun, which are echoed by a pedestal sundial and astrolabe standing in front of the *treillage* screen. The whole paved area of this enclosed garden surrounded a small oblong lily tank where the lilies were said to be flourishing. It is worth noting that Peto shared the view that the water level should be as near to the edge of the pool as possible to give most advantage to the reflection of the surroundings.

Above: *Steps leading down from the summerhouse terrace recall that small feature at Iford, with the steps next to Peto's tea-house.*

Left: *The low-pitched roof of the pavilion, seen here beneath the pleached lime hedge and above the foreshortened canal, emphasises the horizontals of the scene. The lilies, too, have been grown as Peto directed, with enough surface water for the leaves to spread out flat and evenly.*

Adjoining the house on the south-west corner was an open-air summerhouse built in the 1890s to Peto's design, from which a small flight of steps descended to a terrace on the west, with views beneath mature trees to the banks of the River Wey. The simple Tuscan Doric wooden columns supported a high-pitched roof of oak shingles, fitting easily with the house, the roof-line reminiscent of the vernacular tiled roof on the pavilion at Hartham. Cane chairs and cushioned loungers evoke those summer afternoons when tea was taken with views of lawns and distant meadows, while the Japanese ceiling lanterns could have been just a token of the owner's interest in the Eastern arts.

Outside, the simple eighteenth-century-style stone balustrade of Ham Hill stone, built on a low brick retaining wall, enclosed the flagged terrace with paving stones from the Moher cliffs in Ireland (so Tipping tells us). Further flights of steps led down to the western garden and also to the north towards the lily pool. Remarkably, this summerhouse, called 'A garden room', appeared in William Robinson's *English Flower Garden* in 1898, as an example of what he considered to be a 'success' – his view of summerhouses was that they were 'generally a failure and often a heap of decay'. This is a surprising indication that Robinson, the arch defender of the natural gardening school, held Peto in some esteem. In 1903, the planting around this garden room is described in the *Gardeners' Chronicle* as having fragrant climbing roses, honeysuckles, orange trees 'plentifully set with golden fruits', and lilies, pelargoniums and other flowers.

No doubt, then, by 1903 the garden was well planted with borders, shrubs and wild areas, and Peto had already contributed in various ways in the 1890s, making this one of his earliest commissions. By 1908, when the first *Country Life* article was published, a major addition had been put in place only 'two years ago' in this 8-acre garden, one that offered few changes in level to give the garden designer more interesting opportunities – in this respect it shared something with Petwood. The west side of the garden beside the river continued to be developed mainly as a wild garden in the Robinson sense, and the article mentions a sunk garden to which a new brick path had been added and a peat garden for acid-loving plants – andromedas, kalmias, olearias, Menziesias and ericas.

The path continued towards a beech-hedged enclosure for China roses, followed by a rocky dell where 'bulrush and New Zealand flax, Japanese primroses and broad leaved funkias [hostas] revel in what looks like perfectly natural marshland'. At this point the river was reached, which could be crossed by way of the semicircular Japanese bridge designed by Peto in 1905 – one of the few plans in Peto's hand that survives, showing his attention to detail, structural dimensions and wood finishes. The Sumiyoshi Bridge at Osaka, which was illustrated in *Country Life* in 1902, could have inspired his design and his thoughts. 'A bridge is always a consoling object – the spirit crosses it gladly; it is the high road of Fancy, the legitimate pathway of Hope',

Right: *Hydrangeas in full bloom in front of the pavilion, engulfed in Virginia creeper, and irises packed below the quadrant pergolas on either side. The canal lacks the bridge that is at Hartham, but otherwise the core idea is the same.*

Overleaf: *The structural lines of the pleached lime hedge above its bare stems provide a perfect balance between the openness below and enclosure beyond as a hedge screens the distant view.*

wrote Mrs Hugh Fraser in an article on the garden. The bridge was built and survived for the next fifty years, falling into decay only in the 1960s. The alternative to crossing into the meadows was to return to the house along the River Wey, and finally mount the steps to regain the western terrace.

A very different and contrasting experience was planned for the south-eastern corner of the garden. Mature trees surrounded the area and yew hedges were planted to enclose further the 'pleasance', as Tipping called it, and a trellis of rambler roses to screen the croquet ground, so that coming across this enclosure from the rest of the garden was intentionally a surprise. On emerging from the entrance the view was dominated by an arresting canal crossing the lawn, culminating in an imposing pavilion that appeared to float on the water. The focus was concentrated again by a double row of pleached limes, which were planted to make a semicircle around the top of the waterway. Under the limes at their apex, the pavilion stood across the water some 50 yards away. The water would have absorbed the sound and the trees and hedges cut out distant noise, so the scene would have been one of the utmost tranquillity.

The T-shaped canal and the position of the pavilion are a reworking of the designs that were used at Hartham where the Water Garden was also enclosed, in that case by a wall. More comparisons can be drawn, as Tipping does, with the Dutch garden at Westbury Court. The pavilion at Bridge House was very different – more like a Peto loggia than a pavilion – three equal arches over Ionic orders and wide projecting eaves with a shallow-pitched roof of pantiles. Unlike Hartham, where the intention was to create a lofty pavilion, visually necessary to make it stand up above the bridge that ran in front, this pavilion emphasised the horizontal dimension and spread out over the water, keeping the vision floating at eye-level.

The pleached limes further continued the mirage of the stratified plane, which was only broken by the upright tree columns beneath their canopy. As at Hartham, tubbed bays stood on plinths to either side of the arches, but the treatment of the adjoining quadrant colonnades was different: single stone pineapple-topped columns standing at intervals on either side, and linked up with chains, made a curtain of trailing creeper swags. The pavilion looked down the canal over a lead statue of a boy struggling with a serpent and on the corner margins there were two Japanese bronze dragon-toothed fish monsters. The pool and canal were framed with a broad margin of paving stone raised just above the water level and on the other side lapped by the velvety grass sward. This broad central plat was punctuated by standard evergreens in tubs by the water's edge; by contrast, *termini* stood in alcoves in the yew hedges seen under the bare lime tree stems – a row of stilts to support the boxed hedge. Tipping draws attention to the white, chrome, pink and crimson water lilies, with their leaves lying flat on the water, avoiding the tendency to cram in too many plants, which caused their leaves to stick out of the water rather than lying gracefully on it: 'it is water lily growing of the best'.

Avray Tipping seems to have become quite a friend of Seymour Trower; so much so, that when the latter died in 1912, he left him a small legacy. Tipping kept the garden in mind and wrote another article for *Country Life* in 1916. At that time Juliet Trower was still living there, and from the description of the garden it is evident that there had been some important changes made to it since 1908 – it can be assumed that these took place before 1912.

A major structural change in the garden was the building of a substantial wall beginning near the corner of the garden house and running south to divide the wild garden from the more formal areas that have been described. Ostensibly, the wall was built to shelter the plants on the eastern side from the strong south-westerlies blowing up the garden slope from the river. This wall, built in 'brick and stone … in the William III manner', was pierced with arched openings that led through a shady pergola. It offered new formal viewpoints across the centre of the garden (as can be seen in the photographs). Most dramatically a new brick path was built leading to the Water Garden. Along the way, incidents were added – the path focused on a lead statue of the Belvedere Apollo, and then tucked to the left was a Peto temple, six-columned with a wrought-iron roof, in the same mould as the one at Petwood, lacking the statue of Atalanta, but with a finial of decorative iron foliage instead of fleet-footed Mercury. The temple was surrounded by screening shrubbery; it was a place enclosed for contemplation and did not serve as an eye-catcher like the one at Buscot Park.

This was a very special garden of contrasting modes – the Classical and formal features beside the English wild garden with Japanese overtones – but there was no incongruity; the planned structure incorporated shrubs and floriferous screens to avoid any visual competition between the different scenes, and each area was discrete. Avray Tipping finished his article with much extravagant hyperbole: 'not the Garden of Eden of primitive humanity, but the paradise of informed minds that have inherited and absorbed the best traditions of old civilisations and cultured taste.'

Weybridge continued to grow as an overspill suburb for London and the land value of the few acres where the garden was laid out continued to rise. The inevitable happened. At some point in the 1960s, the house was demolished and the site sold for building land. Now, in a leafy estate of small, detached houses, not a trace of Bridge House can be found – the photographs seen here remain as a ghostly reminder of what was once one of Peto's most remarkable gardens.

In contrast to the formal areas, this corner of the garden, with tumbling plants, brick path and a covered arbour, is like a cottage garden.

HEALE HOUSE, WILTSHIRE

Middle Woodford, in Wiltshire, is a small hamlet of cottages scattered along the banks of the Avon, a chalk stream draining from Salisbury Plain, which has over thousands of years created, a lush, fertile valley of water meadows – the kind of land that Hardy's Tess escaped to, so vividly described in the novel, with streams as 'rapid as the shadow of a cloud, with pebbly shallows that prattled to the sky all day long'. In summer burgeoning pastures surround Heale House, which stands nearby, close to the swiftly flowing water. When Peto came here in the early 1900s, he must have been enchanted with what he saw and by the opportunities that were open to him.

At Bridge House and at Hartham, Peto exploited the level sites by giving them the serenity of still pools and canals. At Heale he found a ready-made water garden, for over the centuries the stream had been used to flood the meadows in winter and drain them in the spring.

Above: Detmar Blow's remodelling of the balanced western elevation of the garden front is complemented by Peto's generous approach and the horizontal lines of the cross walks.

Left: Mainly self-set plants soften the broad paved area opposite the south front. It gives ready access to open views over sloping lawns, which are bounded by a wall to the west and the fast-flowing chalk stream beyond.

The irrigation system employed to achieve this was complex, involving the digging of artificial channels (or leats) to raise the water level above the meadow and then others to drain off the water – these were called carriers and drains and formed streams which flowed around the garden. Peto used these features to maximum effect.

The Hon. Louis Greville, who was the brother of Lord Warwick, purchased the house in 1894 while he was still Ambassador to Japan. It is not clear what happened to the house in those early years because family records show that the architect Detmar Blow (1867–1939) was not employed to remodel and extend the house until 1908 and in subsequent years up to 1914. However, the first surviving record of Peto being called in to plan the garden was in 1906. Photographs taken shortly after that show that his plans had been implemented, but that no alterations had taken place on the house, and the old drive running from the south east was still in operation. Louis Greville would have known the work that Peto was doing for his brother at Easton Lodge and most likely that would have prompted the commission at Heale.

The conclusion to be drawn from Peto's plan of January 1906 is that he was only asked to design a rose garden on the island created by the two streams which flowed round the garden. The diamond-shaped island was a substantial size – some 100 yards by 75 yards – and on this Peto designed a footprint of two matching Baroque outlines not unlike the raised moulding of the ceiling panel in the house above the stair hall. The design in the garden was picked out with yew hedges surrounding symmetrically placed rectangular beds, which ran down either side of the cross axis. A centrally placed bridge crossed the stream from the house lawn, and the path led between the parterres and finally up some steps to a garden house on the far side of the island. The plan shows pergolas stretching out along the banks to either side of the building.

An aerial photograph taken about eight years later shows the yew hedges well grown, the pattern of beds in place, but no evidence that the garden house or the pergola were ever built. Today, as this part of the garden has gone back to the wild, the formality of such a rose garden in the middle of meandering streams may seem incongruous. Peto chose to conceal the geometric parterre with yew hedges so that the eye would only see the curving hedge outlines, complementing the water flowing around the island.

There were two important features in the garden that apparently predated the design of the Rose Garden – the Japanese bridge and the tea-house. Both of these are included on Peto's 1906 plan and the Greville family tradition says that he had no hand in the construction of either of them. Louis Greville was employed for many years in the diplomatic service in Tokyo, and according to family history he imported both features from Japan, the bridge being a copy of the one at Nikko, and it is said that he even employed Japanese carpenters to undertake the reconstruction on site. Certainly it is evident that both objects were at least conceived by 1906. Wherever the inspiration for them came from, it is worth recalling that Peto had designed the Japanese bridge for the Seymour Trowers in 1905 and the tea-house for Easton Lodge a little before that. At Heale, the siting of both the bridge and the tea-house were critical. The 'Nikko' bridge, a gently curving structure leaping the water, gave immediate access to the island from the southern end, but prior to 1906 there was no Rose Garden to visit, which begs the question of what was there before Peto's plan. The position of the tea-house was a fascinating choice too. It stands precisely over the place where the two streams cross and this is achieved – essential if the irrigation system was to continue working – by the one being carried over the other on an aqueduct.

As regards the layout of the garden it is not clear what happened over the five years prior to the plans that were drawn up by Peto in May 1911. The records show that Detmar Blow was at work on the house from 1908, and the extensive work that he was to carry out had serious implications for the garden. It is a matter of conjecture whether the two men discussed the alterations so that Peto's new

Continuing the symmetry and balance of the seventeenth-century-style house, the central path arrives at the cross-terrace which matches the width of the house. A large planted copper on a millstone provides the pivotal feature, typical of an Arts and Crafts garden. Peto's preference on the plan was for a statue at the focal point.

garden would complement the altered elevations, but whatever the formal arrangement, in reality there must have been a large degree of cooperation. The overall plan of 1911 shows the existing footprint of the house (whether built or not by that date), the planning of new gardens to the south and west, and most importantly that the drive to the south has been re-routed, thus clearing the way for the new garden to be planned in the elbow of the streams. Detmar Blow had in effect turned the house round and a new entrance front was created on the north side. Peto's plan shows a semicircular forecourt to accompany the new elevation, and then the drive striking east, crossing the streams and turning south to meet up with the old drive far beyond the confines of the garden. It was this re-orientation of the house that so spectacularly opened up fresh possibilities to make new gardens on the east and to the south. The alterations to the house and garden were firmly dovetailed together.

The garden that Peto planned opposite the remodelled south wing was now free of the drive and bounded by the irrigation streams to the east and to the south, and the stables and a wall to the west. The ground sloped gradually down to the streambank with the view from the house being kept clear, over the lawn to the distant Rose Garden on the island. The main architectural features to be planned were the 'landing' and the garden house, both tucked away against the stream

on the east. In the lower half of this garden, Peto planned a 'Panel Garden'. A rectangular plot with an apsidal end, the shape was levelled and the form defined with a low retaining wall on the top side and an 18-inch-high box hedge on the lower side, with openings punctuated with 'upright box'. The garden was laid out with a panel of equal-sized rectangular beds down each side of the 'aisle'. No planting plans survive. The retaining wall is still in place but no indication whether the Panel Garden was ever planted.

On the line of the cross axis running parallel to and above the Panel Garden, Peto had planned a garden house to the east with its back to the stream; an open-fronted, three-arched loggia with stone Tuscan Doric columns, built with stone quoins in the same style as the house. The elevation plan is very similar to the pavilion at Bridge House – also triple arcaded – but at Heale a steeper roof pitch was designed in keeping with the main house. The garden house would have faced south looking across the Panel Garden to the river and the Rose Garden island beyond – though there is no evidence that this building was ever constructed.

Right: *The wide, paved cross-terrace, spanning the garden, is well hedged with roses and standard wisterias, and sealed off at either end with a curving stone exedra, quite unlike the Roman examples Peto used elsewhere.*

Below: *Peto built this little 'boat' terrace so as to be as close to the water as possible. It is surrounded with a finely crafted balustrade to give prominence to its association with the stream.*

Just upstream from the planned site of the garden house, on the flank of Detmar Blow's east wing, is a little incident of immeasurable success – perhaps the most magical of them all. The sight of the clear flowing chalk streams, with their trailing mats of emerald vegetation and trout darting through the current, must have been an enduring delight for Peto, and he simply wanted to build a feature that would bring these pleasurable visions right to your feet. The bank stood about 5 feet above the stream and he designed a 'landing' right at the water's edge where he could have imagined, as in Tennyson's poem, the Lady of Shallot departing for Camelot. The view across the lawn from the house is bounded by a low seventeenth-century-style balustrade of Chilmark stone, which stands above the excavated landing, and at each end steps descend from the lawn with a sloping balustrade beside the stream. These balusters complement the ones on the stairs in the house. Once down on the landing there are a few clear yards where one can trail ones hand in the crystal water. This intimate contact with the water evokes the breaks in the balustrade at Easton where water and viewer meet. Today, in summer the exotic leaves of *Gunnera manicata* spread out over the stream from the opposite bank

and the balustrade is covered in rambling roses. Lady Anne Rasch, who lived at Heale and made so many fine additions to the garden, said in the guide book that some of the ramblers were 'legacies from 1920 with long-forgotten names, but exceptionally long-flowering, and greatly valued'. This invites us to reflect whether the roses were the very ones recommended and planted to the original design by Peto.

The western elevation, sometimes called the garden front, is the most balanced and harmonious of the restorations, half of it dating from the early house – probably seventeenth-century – and the other half built by Detmar Blow to provide a match so perfect that it is almost impossible to tell the new from the old. The central door, with projecting gabled bays on either side, each with uniform niches, seems to require that the garden laid out on the gentle western slope should reflect the symmetry and make a grand sequel to the house. This is what it does.

A broad flagged path leads directly from the garden door, continuing up the slope, dividing what is nearly a square into two equal halves, and joining the top terrace that holds both halves together. The paved level area immediately in front of the house, divided off with a balustrade of the same design as the one on the river walk, serves as a springboard to the large sloping central garden. This level area is bisected with paths that run parallel to the house, the first of which forms a north-south axis running down to the river. In this paved court, Peto planned a central fountain and to either side rectangular beds with vases. This is not confirmed by the earliest photographs of 1915, which show a sundial in the middle and plain turfed panels on either side. At some later date, probably not to Peto's design, two ornate, oval lily pools were built in place of the turf. The axial path led out of the court up a small flight of steps through the balustrade to either side of which were once mounted awesome Greek gladiators in combat.

The whole central thrust of the garden was maintained by a row of laburnums on either side, leading to the top terrace which was reached by another short flight of steps. A statue on the plan was placed as a focal point from the house and now replaced by a copper filled with plants. This strong cross axis, serving as a bridge on which to take bearings and regard the house, echoes the design of Petwood. The broad paved bridge is terminated at either end by curved seats and standard wisterias, which formed the dominant planting on either side, thus to some extent enclosing the vista and focusing on the end seats. Down the north side of the garden, banks of flowering shrubs were planted effectively to screen the drive that ran behind to the new north entrance.

Inevitably, the herbaceous planting schemes have changed over the years and much new garden has been very successfully added, particularly in the kitchen garden area – an enchanting apple tunnel, or arbour, and tightly clipped box balls arranged at the corners of the central dipping tank – said to be planted in the Edwardian era and therefore possibly Peto's idea. Near the Japanese tea-house there is a fine *Cercidiphyllum*, the Katsura tree, which was introduced to this country from Japan around the beginning of the twentieth century. Quite possibly Louis Greville planted this tree when making the Japanese garden at Heale, but it is surely no coincidence that there is another specimen at Iford Manor. One planting must have inspired the other and it is likely that Peto imported his, as he did many other plants from Japan after his voyage there in 1898.

This garden remains near its water meadows and the stream is still the boundary of most of the southern garden. It is evident that Peto did not want to disturb this natural order and his designs reflect this *modus operandi* – it feels like a flat valley landscape where the dominant lines are horizontal and the swiftly flowing streams form the contour lines. Even the air floats like a mirage over the fields. How much of the irrigation system with carriers and drains served a practical purpose will never be clear, but what is unforgettable is the way the waterways have been used to enhance the pleasure of the garden experience.

After years in the diplomatic service in Tokyo, the Hon. Louis Greville was so impressed by Japanese culture that he imported this tea-house, and had it erected at Heale House around 1906, when Peto was first invited to plan the garden.

Above: This view through the sliding panels of the tea-house frames the bridge, and gives a glimpse of the walled garden and the former farm buildings beyond.

Left: The Japanese bridge, a copy of the one at Nikko, was constructed close to the tea-house and gave access to Peto's Rose Garden, which was entirely surrounded by streams.

WAYFORD MANOR & BURTON PYNSENT, SOMERSET

When there is an architect in the family, he or she is often called upon to give advice when it comes to buying, renovating or landscaping a new domain. Harold Peto, as one of fourteen children, had frequent requests for help in these matters from his siblings, and in some cases he was asked to draw up quite considerable garden schemes. Two of these in the West Country were for his sisters, a younger one, Helen, at Wayford Manor, and an elder sister, Sarah, at Burton Pynsent.

Helen Peto had married Ingham Baker in 1885, and after early-married life in Middlesex they bought Wayford Manor in the late 1890s. One of the attractions of the West Country may have been to be nearer Helen's eldest brother Sir Henry, who had bought in 1893

Wayford Manor, Somerset: (above) The long terrace that Peto designed for his sister stretches right across the width of the main garden. Peto's three-arched loggia, which is a virtual copy of the Elizabethan entrance porch, can be seen here adjoining the south-facing front of the house.

(left): *Clipped yew hedges enclose a bronze statue of Mercury in the Iris Garden.*

an estate at Chedington, Dorset, some five miles to the east. Helen's sister Edith moved into Seaborough Court, only a few miles away from Wayford around 1904; and yet another sister Sarah, who had married into the Crossley family, also came to live nearby, moving to Burton Pynsent near Langport in 1909. All three sisters were very close to each other and to Harold; they were regular visitors at Iford over the next thirty years, and towards the end of Peto's life, it was Helen and Sarah who visited most frequently. It was probably Helen who was with him when he died.

Living nearby, it is no surprise that Peto developed schemes for his sisters' gardens in particular at Wayford and Burton Pynsent, which by coincidence were both built on ridges to the south and east of the Taunton plain. Both sat on the edge of the steep slope and had magnificent views: Burton Pynsent to the north and Wayford to the south. Peto took full advantage of this. Both schemes were simple, but Wayford was the more ambitious of the two.

Wayford Manor has a typical E-shaped plan, with the date 1602 on the library chimneypiece; it has all the outward characteristics of an Elizabethan manor although it has a medieval core. When the Bakers came to Wayford the existing northern wing had not yet been built, so they employed Ernest George and his new partner Alfred Yeates in 1901–02 to complete what had clearly been the unfulfilled ambition of the Daubeney family in 1600: the construction of the north wing to balance the existing seventeenth-century one. Most striking is the central triple-arched entrance loggia that in its conformity echoes the south porch at Cranborne Manor, Dorset – both have an elaborate frieze, slightly wider central opening and arches of raised alternate voussoirs, with Tudor roses carved between them. It was typical of innovations of the time to incorporate quasi-Renaissance features into older buildings.

Peto must have been working on the garden after the construction of the new wing, which both enclosed and gave a comfortable symmetry to the entrance courtyard. He further surrounded this with a low wall to the west, and a yew hedge to the south. The central porch was approached through an opening in the wall, framed by short ball-topped piers. A broad flagged path led between standard Portugal laurels to the loggia – a restrained piece of design, which complements the Elizabethan exterior perfectly and emphasises the vernacular traditions adhered to by the Arts and Crafts architects.

The outer forecourt has features created with yew topiary to make – in the Jekyll sense – garden rooms, one of which immediately opposite the paved approach is a U-shaped hedge surrounding a fine copy of a Byzantine font from Ravenna, which is the focal point from the loggia. More architectural yews make a hidden courtyard next to the farm buildings, where a copy of the bronze statue of Giambologna's Mercury on a pedestal is complemented by beds of tall-bearded irises – Mercury, like the goddess Iris, was the messenger

Wayford Manor, Somerset: The hidden walled garden (right), *with access down the stairs from the main terrace, surrounds a large rectangular pool, over-shadowed by* Acer palmatum. *At the side stands a copy of one of Peto's favourite* amorino *fountains from Pompeii. The wall opening leads out to the lower terrace from which there is a view back up to the house along the garden axis* (above).

of the gods and descended to earth on a rainbow. One hundred-
year-old Italian cypresses still stand in the sandy courtyard making it
all for a moment seem like Tuscany. This yard, closed off by the house
at one end and by the farm buildings at the other, has a great yew
hedge barrier along the south, concealing the dramatic view that lies
beyond.

At the corner of the house a small path, aligned on the main axis of
the garden, leads through this massive yew hedge to the first terrace,
revealing the surprise position of the house on the crest of the slope,
and a view over the River Axe to the Dorset hills (now much hidden
by large trees). This terrace, long, narrow and paved with a rustic
garden house at the west end, overlooking a rectangular pool headed
by one of Peto's favourite fountains, an *amorino* with a dolphin, is
shaded by a massive horse chestnut dominating the terrace a few steps
below. This tree is on the main terrace, an Elizabethan bowling lawn
that embraces the width of the garden from Peto's three-arched loggia

Burton Pynsent, Somerset: (left) This garden was designed by Peto for his elder sister, Sarah
Crossley. In typical fashion, he built up the terrace opposite the eastern façade to take advantage
of the magnificent views over the eighteenth-century parkland towards William Pitt's monument
to his benefactor, Sir William Pynsent.

(above): *Beyond the east terrace one of the remaining cedar trees, planted by Pitt, is still*
flourishing. Other cedars planted too near to the house were removed to open up the view.

(built on the side of the house and almost a copy of the entrance
porch) to the other end dominated by the shade of the giant chestnut.
It is said that fragments of an earlier balustrade were recovered from
the garden and Peto used these to draw the sketch, now at Dumbarton
Oaks, from which the Ham Hill balustrade was turned. This terrace,
with its reputedly Elizabethan steps, is probably all that remains of the
earlier garden.

Continuing down the stairway on the main axis of the garden,
another lower terrace with flowery borders slopes gently down to
more steps, which descend to an even lower garden, sometimes called
the 'wild garden'. Beside the path a magnolia, *Magnolia x Soulangeana*,
dating from Peto's scheme, overshadows another pool, and is a
preparation for the incidents of Japanese landscaping that lie beyond.
At the western end of this terrace the path disappears through a doorway to a hidden garden, walled on all sides, with a pool for contemplation and a large *Acer palmatum* shading the water – another touch
of the East. From the corner of this area, a balustraded stairway
ascends to the main terrace beneath the boughs of the great chestnut.

On the sloping lower terrace the view of the garden below is one of
winding paths, profusely planted – some of the plants, such as the
Betula Maximowicziana first introduced from Japan in 1893, could be

from the Peto planting, as could the large and handsome pines, *Pinus pinaster* and *Pinus radiata*, which stand on either side of the garden just below the terrace. Humphrey Baker (Helen's son) took a keen interest in the garden that he inherited, knowing that the acid greensand soil provided good lime-free growing conditions. He was able to add many new species to this naturally planted 'wild' area of the garden, as have the present owners, making it today a mature garden of both exciting formal and natural planting.

Of all Peto's garden schemes the one at Wayford seems comparable to Iford; the situation is similar except the house here is at the top of the slope rather than at the bottom. The overall shape is different: Iford is broadly across the slope, while at Wayford the main part of the garden runs down the slope, with tennis courts and separate garden areas off to either side. Wayford was planned to have its formal areas around the forecourt and on the terraces, leading to the natural garden below. At Iford the formal areas have been planned round the edges, leaving the centre more freely planted, to include rocks and runnels of water in the Japanese manner.

Burton Pynsent has grand associations. It was lived in and enlarged by the fortunate William Pitt, Earl of Chatham, who had it bequeathed to him by an admiring countryman, Sir William Pynsent, in 1765. What remains from the eighteenth century is a rolling landscape, attributed to Capability Brown, sweeping along the hillside to the east in the direction of Pitt's tower. This was built as a memorial in gratitude to his benefactor, to be seen from the house and admired from afar. When the widowed Sarah Crossley bought the house in 1909, perhaps to be closer to her sister Helen, early photographs show there was hardly any garden at all around the dwelling. On the eastern side the ground fell away, with magnificent views over Sedgemoor, and here Pitt had misguidedly planted Lebanon cedars (thinking they would be dwarf conifers perhaps), some of which had survived, far too close to the house, which they entirely overshadowed.

Burton Pynsent, Somerset: (above) The clipped Portugal laurels and fastigiate yews create the vista viewed across the east front.

(left): This view over the long lawn, framed by a utilitarian pergola (rather uncharacteristic of Peto), is given form by the mushroom-topped laurels, and centred on one of the eighteenth-century cedars of Lebanon.

Peto, who was consulted early on, saw the potential of the views towards Pynsent's monument, and accordingly replaced the large cedars with a balustraded terrace, which perfectly matched the proportions of the façade. This east elevation was altered and given a handsome central doorway, with a short flight of semicircular steps descending to an axial paved path which bisected the terrace before reaching a wrought-iron gate in the middle of the terrace balustrade, from which steps led down to the lower garden. It is quite simple, and the *Country Life* photographs of 1934 show large box buttons punctuating the corners beside the path.

On the west, Sarah Crossley built a large, Baroque gabled entrance front, with a central Venetian window and a triple-arched rustic loggia below, which opened onto an enormous carriage drive. It is very doubtful that this was Peto's design. A rather dull conservatory wing was thrown out to the south and extends as a wall, hiding the garden scheme that Peto developed to the south east of the house. Very discreetly, a nicely proportioned Arts and Crafts doorway, aligned on the garden axis, leads from the driveway into the pergola. Here, there is a striking view down the flagged path to a long panel garden, with a surviving Pitt cedar in its maturity as the distant focal point. Simplicity was the keynote; large domed box bushes and mushroom-topped Portugal laurels mark the way and offset the nearside of a gigantic hedge enclosing the lawn. The pergola, too, is simple and for Peto unusually utilitarian, with no Tuscan columns this time, but unadorned brick columns instead, with blunt-ended oak beams across the top.

Most charming of all is the lime tree walk, which outstrips the length of the plat lawn on the south side behind the yew hedge. It is described as 'a pleached lime avenue' in *Country Life* 1934, but this is rather an exaggeration as today there is no evidence of pleaching as such, but rather of regular pruning to maintain bush tops (pollards) which in themselves form sculpture in winter and provide shade when in leaf.

In the 1930s, the garden was looking mature and, in this simple form, at its best. It has none of the extravaganzas of some of Peto's other commissions; most likely his sister wanted it that way. Sarah Crossley was very elderly by 1934 when the garden was photographed, and she died in 1938.

Burton Pynsent, Somerset: An avenue of young lime trees runs parallel to the long lawn, with a glimpse of the east façade seen over the hedge. Most likely Peto was planning to pleach the limes to make a box hedge on bare stems, as at Bridge House.

3:
Ilnacullin:
Ireland's
Riviera

Above: *One of the bonsai trees at Ilnacullin, a Japanese larch, (*Larix kæmpferi*).*

Left: *From this position on the highest point of the island – the site of the Martello tower – there is just a glimpse of the* campanile-*style Clock Tower and the casita. A small window between the trees, overlooks the bay and the outline of the Caha Mountains.*

An island garden brings to mind a dream of paradise and erotic love as it did for Poliphilo, the hero of the famous Renaissance story *The Strife of Love in a Dream* (*Hypnerotomachia Poliphili*), published in Venice in 1499. Poliphilo, while searching for his beloved Polia on the island of Cytherea, is intrigued by the ruins of antiquity, which become objects of his worship, described in many detailed and elaborate evocations of fantastic architectural garden forms. This narrative and its exquisite illustrations have influenced garden designers through the ages. When Harold Peto had the opportunity to make an island garden, it must have seemed a heaven-sent gift.

However, on the day Peto first looked out at Garinish Island he would not have found it exactly promising: rocky, bleak, treeless, overgrown with gorse and heather, and allegedly populated only by goats. The island is about 37 acres in area, and sits at the mouth of Glengarriff Harbour at the northern end of Bantry Bay. Known locally as Garinish Island, meaning the near island, it lies only a few hundred yards off the shores of Glengarriff village. In the early nineteenth century, because of its strategic position, a Martello tower was built on the highest rock to defend the harbour against a Napoleonic invasion. The British War Office continued to exercise control over the island until the beginning of the twentieth century, although the tower had long before been abandoned.

When the Belfast born Annan Bryce (1843–1923), younger son of the Scot and geologist James Bryce, visited Bantry Bay at the end of the nineteenth century he would have seen Garinish Island in its barren, natural state. Nevertheless, he and his wife, Violet, developed a passion for the area and regularly stayed at Glengarriff Castle for the summer season. In 1909, Mrs Bryce writing in the local newspaper, *The Throne and Country*, about the appeal of Glengarriff, referred to it as 'one of the most beautiful holiday resorts in the United Kingdom'. She listed the many and varied attractions, including boating, mountain climbing and sketching, claiming that few places enjoyed such superb weather. She called it 'Ireland's Riviera'. No wonder the Bryces wanted somewhere in the area to settle.

Annan Bryce had worked in Asia for much of his early life, leading adventurous journeys into unknown areas of Burma, taking a particular interest in plants, and writing up these expeditions as papers for

Above: The Clock Tower, today, surrounded by luxuriant planting; in 1910, it was just bare rock and scrub.

Right: Nature and art. This open, balanced pavilion is poised to look both ways: inwards to the formal pool of the sunk garden and outwards, as in this view, to the rocky slopes of Sugarloaf Mountain.

Overleaf: The statue of Mercury stands at the centre of the pool, as if the gods had come to earth to make this iconic image of Peto's elegant pavilion reflected in the water, surrounded by great trees and mountains. The Japanese bonsai plants in ancient pots, at either end, play on the dichotomy between artifice and nature.

the Royal Geographical Society. He retired from India in 1883. After that, his enthusiasm for the southern Irish coast must have been stimulated by the realisation that the equable climate provided the ideal growing conditions for a wide range of exotic and subtropical plants. Visiting existing gardens in the locality gave him proof of this.

In a letter to his brother, written from Glengarriff Castle in August 1905, he recounts that while on the steamer near Cork he ran into Harold Peto, who took him to visit gardens in the neighbourhood. One of them was the garden of 'a local brewer, Beamish', which was famous as an alpine garden that had been made in an old quarry, 'with really beautiful results'. Another was 'the famous garden of Smith Barry' on Fota Island in the tidal estuary of the River Lee, 8 miles from Cork. Hugh Smith Barry (1816–57) had carried out much of the groundwork here, which included planting a 15-acre arboretum. It was his son, later Lord Barrymore, who continued to make Fota one of the most important collections of plants in Ireland. Annan Bryce admired the bamboos, which 'are flowering for the first time after 30 years', and especially the tree ferns, and also the rare conifers which have 'mostly been in about 60 years and have attained the height of 50 or 60 feet'. Of the cut-leaf beech, or the pinnatifid Oriental plane, he advises his brother to 'get specimens of these, neither of which you have'. It is clear from this correspondence that both brothers were keenly interested in plants; there is another letter in 1914, which refers to their interest in the latest book to be written by 'Chinese' Wilson, the great collector of plants, *A Naturalist in Western China* (1913). There is also correspondence between the Bryces and Sir Joseph Hooker, the former Director of Kew Gardens.

Annan Bryce on his regular summer visits to Glengarriff must have looked longingly at the collections of plants that he found at Fota, Birr Castle, Annes Grove, and other gardens, and realised that at Garinish Island across the harbour there was the possibility of creating another island paradise. His wife was also enthusiastic, for she wanted to help the local community; she wrote much later, in 1929, that the idea of buying Garinish had been 'with a view to making gardens and building a house, and giving employment to the large and poor population living up the glens, the district being what is called "congested" – that is, the land is too poor to make a living off.' When the British War Office decided to sell the island, which it had owned for over a hundred years, the Bryces had the chance they had been waiting for, and it was conveyed to Annan Bryce in August 1910.

It is inconceivable that Bryce had not talked to Peto over the years about his desire to make a garden in that region, which had been their holiday home for so many summers. They had long been friends. Peto's visitors' book records that Annan and Violet first stayed with him in 1896, when he was at Landford House, near Salisbury, and then regularly at Iford Manor from 1904 to 1912 – the children accompanying their parents in 1911 and 1912. Quite probably these visits were reciprocated, with Peto visiting the Bryces at Glengarriff, particularly in the crucial phase when they were thinking of buying the island. So when Peto was finally asked to draw up plans, he would already have been familiar with the landscape of the island and with Annan's enthusiasm for plants. For his part, Bryce would have seen

the developments at Iford Manor and appreciated Peto's skill in handling garden architecture.

Bryce would undoubtedly also have been familiar with some of Peto's other commissions, particularly Hartham Park, which is only a few miles from Iford. It could well have been the object of a weekend's excursion, which is why it is no coincidence that the garden pavilion at Garinish is so similar to the one at Hartham. Moreover, with Henry Seymour Trower living at No. 9 Bryanston Square in London and Annan Bryce at No. 35, both close friends of Peto and both very interested in making gardens, the pavilion at Trower's Bridge House, standing at the head of the canal would also have been familiar to the Bryces. The idea of a pavilion presiding over the sunk garden at Ilnacullin was a seed waiting to be planted.

The plan for Garinish Island appeared to flow effortlessly from Peto's mind, for Mrs Annan Bryce wrote in the 1920s: 'He went up to the Martello tower from whence it is possible to see most of the island, and, waving his magic wand, produced what is undoubtedly one of the most beautiful gardens of the world.' At this stage, in the autumn of 1910, photographs of the island still show a rocky outcrop, practically barren, save for low-growing scrub and gorse, treeless, with the remains of the early nineteenth-century battlements surrounding the Martello tower on the ridge of rocks on the south-east side of the island. The Bryces had not only commissioned Peto to design the garden, but in addition to build a palatial house on the site of the Martello tower for which plans were also prepared. The garden layout shows immediately that Peto had accepted his brief with due respect for the wishes of his clients, who said 'they carried out his plan with only minor alterations'.

A formal area in the best of Peto's architectural style, which Bryce, being so familiar with his work, must have wanted, is the core of the plan, and slowly structural lines spread out from there, embracing and complementing the natural features to provide suitable zones for wild and subtropical planting. The structured axis runs on level ground

Above: *This capital on one of the columns of the casita, or garden house, is almost identical to the ones Peto designed for West Dean. They all date from 1911–12.*

Right: *The casita faces the rectangular pool, which is surrounded by tiles and 'map-paving', in the formal sunk garden.*

from south west to north east, covering about three-quarters of the length of the island, starting with the sunk garden (now named the Italian Garden) in the south, through an area of spacious lawns, which were for croquet and tennis, and then to the walled kitchen garden, taking the axis through the middle of a long rectangular plot. The formal areas were planned to extend further along this axis, with a rose garden at the east end of the island, but this was never fully constructed. For the other half of the island Peto designed another axis, following the features and contours of the ground, with sweeping paths leading through naturally planted areas in the style so favoured by William Robinson.

It is often said that this garden was the marriage of two minds – Peto with his Italian dream and Bryce with his vision of a tropical paradise. While it is undoubtedly true that Bryce must have contributed enormously to the selection of plants, the plan shows Peto's

readiness and acumen to unify both coherently. There is constant attention to good structure, for the seemingly wild areas have been brilliantly held together by the subsidiary axis (running more or less parallel to the formal one), which was shaped by the long glade of the 'Happy Valley'. This glade had steps at one end leading to the temple, and at the other steps mounting the rock to the Martello tower, where the house was planned to be. Peto grasped the opportunity to create a wonderful 'wild' garden, structured in the manner of the natural gardens of Japan, and he knew his client, inspired by Fota and other Irish gardens, fostered ambitions to grow foreign species.

When Annan Bryce bought the island in 1910 it was known as Garinish Island, but he discovered it had another name in old Gaelic: Ilnacullin, meaning 'island of holly'. Believing this to be the much older name, Bryce decided to adopt it with the consequence that today, rather confusingly, the garden is known by both names. (Generally, if the garden is being referred to then 'Ilnacullin' is used, though Garinish Island still appears on official maps). Plans for the island were prepared at the end of 1910, and according to *The Irish Builder and Engineer* work was underway by April of the following year and continued for three years until the outbreak of war, with a

Left: *The grand entrance to a large walled kitchen garden, which would have been essential as Annan Bryce intended to build an Italian palazzo and live on the island. This view looks back to the garden house, or, as it was called later, the casita.*

Below: *Spectacular herbaceous borders form the principal feature along the central path of the walled garden.*

hundred men being employed and vast quantities of soil being brought from the mainland.

At a different Garinish Island, in Co. Kerry, the 3rd Earl of Dunraven had done the same in the late nineteenth century, importing large amounts of soil to improve the fertility. Both Bryce and Peto would have appreciated the need to develop shelterbelts before more ambitious planting was carried out. There were precedents at nearby Rossdohan, an island in one of Co. Kerry's deep inlets, where a retired Surgeon-Major, Samuel Heard, had planted a garden. On this island, far less protected from the Atlantic gales than Garinish (Ilnacullin), his first consideration had been to plant windbreaks after he acquired the island in 1870. There were other examples, too, such as Fota, where Smith Barry had planted shelterbelts against the westerlies, and the exposed position of Tresco Abbey in the Isles of Scilly – which would have been familiar at least to Bryce – where trees had been planted in the nineteenth century to protect the new subtropical planting.

The lack of soil and protection from the wind were two of the primary concerns in laying the foundations for Ilnacullin. Where there was too much exposed rock in areas that had to be levelled or planted, Peto's plan required the blasting of rock and there were other areas on the plan where the soil could be quarried. The sheltering trees were planted around the shores of the island against the prevailing winds, and were mainly coniferous – Austrian and Scotch pines, *Pinus montana* and *Pinus insignis* (Monterey pine) were all stipulated on Peto's drawing.

The architectural form of the garden must have been completed in these initial years – the garden house, the sunk garden and the pavilion would all have been built by 1914 – for during the War garden and building labour would not have been available, and according to Mrs Bryce only maintenance was carried out. Immediately after the War, however, there was, according to the planting records, a burst of activity in 1919, with hundreds of new species being introduced to the island. After that, planting activity appears to have tailed off. By this stage Annan Bryce had already spent a large fortune on the garden, and his financial circumstances would have been adversely affected by the collapse of the Russian market after 1917. He was now in his seventies, retired from active politics and in failing health; he died four years later in 1923.

His widow says very little about Ilnacullin at this crucial time after the War and evidence about the garden is very scanty, but following her husband's death she moved to Garinish, where she lived in one of the small cottages, keen to take an interest in local life, although she still kept her house in Bryanston Square. In 1928, she advertised for, and later appointed, a Scottish head gardener, which led to the long and successful career of Murdo Mackenzie. He came from a gardening family and much later recounted that no planting was done in the garden for three years after his arrival; instead he and three under gardeners spent 'everyday cleaning the windbreaks, architectural

Peto designed a long open glade, which he called 'Happy Valley' on the plan. It gave the opportunity for the natural planting of the rich subtropical flora that Annan Bryce envisaged for his cherished island garden.

features and plants' of the overgrowth of weeds. This would seem to suggest that the garden had been in a state of decline at least after the death of Bryce, but readily confirms that all the architectural elements in the Italian Garden had been built.

However, a slightly different picture emerges from the descriptions and photographs of the garden in the later 1920s, which show the garden more or less in hand. The next major change was that Mrs Bryce's son, Roland, came to live on the island with her in 1932 and began to develop the planting with Murdo Mackenzie during the 1930s. Mrs Bryce died in 1939 and Roland inherited the island. He continued to live there until his death in 1953. Under the terms of his will he left the garden to the Irish state and it was put under the control of the then Commissioners of Public Works. Mackenzie continued to be the gardener at Ilnacullin until he retired in the late 1960s, but remained on the island in his retirement. The horticultural diversity and richness that is there today must in part reflect the period when Roland Bryce and Mackenzie worked together on the subtropical planting.

Taking the boat over the short stretch of water from the harbour village of Glengarriff to the island is already an enchanting experience. One passes rocky outcrops and basking seals before reaching the new landing slip on the northern sheltered shore. The formal structured axis lies just 100 yards ahead, the path leading beside the north bed, which is now planted with tender acacias and spring flowering magnolia and sheltered by the pines from Peto's plan. Central to this wild natural planting is Peto's sunk garden, surrounded by yew hedges and shrubs on two sides, with the garden house, or casita, to the east and the open pavilion to the west. This is the jewel of the garden created in a wild landscape that makes for a deeper appreciation of both civilised formality and natural wildness.

The steps from the landing slip bring you in at the corner of the casita (Peto called it the garden house). Arriving at the central point, the view extends over the pool and a statue of Mercury, up the steps on the far side, through the central arch of the small pavilion with a view towards the Caha Mountains. This perfectly balanced and secluded perspective, which has taken central stage on so many of Ireland's garden publications, stands as a remarkable symbol for harmony between the formal and the wild. The pavilion was called the Medici House by the American garden writer Rose Nichols in 1929, because the columns and arch suggest that its inspiration came from the Villa di Papa Giulio in Rome, which overlooks a sunken water-court, and was familiar to Peto. Here, it combines features of both the Hartham and Bridge House pavilions – Hartham with the high central arch but not its high roof, and Bridge with its shallowly-pitched roof reminiscent of traditional Japanese garden buildings. There are more hints of the Japanese style with bonsai trees in pots, which so fascinated Peto when he was in the East in 1898, and which he imported for Iford and undoubtedly for Bryce also. One of the bonsai trees at Ilnacullin, a fine *Larix*, is said to be nearly 300 years old. The pavilion of Bath stone has a roof which ingeniously

The steps at the end of Happy Valley lead up to the Martello tower.

complements the distant Sugarloaf Mountain. The Mediterranean is brought to mind as the distant view is framed between pink *rosso antico* columns, celebrated in the time of the Roman Empire, lost and subsequently rediscovered.

As one turns away from the bay and the mountains and looks back over the pool to the east, the view is sealed off by another colonnaded garden building, looking as if it were the proud and sturdy parent of the small pavilion, its young and elegant offspring. Another continent comes crowding into the scene: the design of the casita is taken from the Spanish Charles V pavilion in the Alcázar gardens in Seville. Peto first visited these originally Moorish gardens on his trip to Spain in 1888. Later he made a small drawing, preserved in the Dumbarton Oaks archive, which shows that he clearly intended to use the building in a design, for he drew round windows on the squat tower above the loggia, or verandah, with a note saying, '? make windows for light'. That is exactly what he did at Ilnacullin, but he restructured the ground floor with columns supporting beams, whereas the Spanish pavilion has a colonnade with arches supporting the loggia roof – the central door to the inside is the same. At Ilnacullin, Peto added a colonnaded verandah with wings to either side. In an article in *The Cork Examiner* of 1933, the casita was described as being built of 'Bath stone', the pillars supporting solid beams of teak 'weathered to the

colour of Bath stone', the inside walls 'panelled with slabs of marble from the island of Scyros, set in Carrara marble' and the floor 'of green Connemara marble'. Peto had created an amalgam of different cultural designs and materials.

Turning back once more to look at the infant pavilion the whole scene is brought to focus on the blue-tiled pool made to reflect the sky – not for Peto a dark lily pond here, but rather an echo of those brightly tiled Moorish pools, which he saw in the Alhambra and the courtyards of Tangier on his trip 'to get a peep at the gorgeous East'. At the pivotal point there is a statue of the flying Mercury, subject of so many Greek myths and for Peto a favourite figure, seen also on the temple at Petwood and in the Iris Garden at Peto's sister's house, Wayford Manor. Peto loved all the myths of course, but most of all the poise and balance of the pointing figure, in the same way that he had admired, and so often copied, the dancing faun from Pompeii.

The pool surround too is a new departure – not in this case the coursed paving flags that surround the canals at Hartham and Bridge

Above: Was the intention ever to roof this temple? The site that Peto chose for it on this rocky promontory must have brought to mind the ruined temples of Greece.

Right: The enduring view of Bantry Bay and the rugged coastline of the Beara peninsula from the temple promontory. It accentuates the juxtaposition of the wildness of the surrounding landscape and this jewel set in an island paradise.

House, but 'map-paving', as he liked to call it, which he used for the pergola at West Dean. For Ilnacullin's exotic location Peto wanted to avoid the look of stone paving which pushes the distance away with its perspective grid, and decided instead to create a mosaic of different shapes to diffuse attention, letting the blue pool float. In the detailing of the surround he combined ceramic tiles on edge and other materials to provide patterns of circles and octagons. These in their turn marked the positions for standing columns and other sculptural objects characteristic of the way in which Peto loved to make allusions to antiquity.

Raised terraces surround the pool, with flights of steps ascending from the mid-point on each side, as at Petwood, and in 1929 it was described as having borders 'planted chiefly with gay flowering shrubs, and annuals such as salmon-rose begonias, pink and yellow snapdragons, and pansies of the richest purple. From Australia was imported the *Callistemon lanceolatus* with its flaming cardinal-red blossoms; from New Zealand, several varieties of Leptospermum with white, pink and dark red flowers.' The shrubs included Asiatic azaleas and white rhododendrons from the Himalayas. Cypresses and bay laurels growing in tubs provided the definitive accents. Today, some of these accents are no longer there but the emphasis on this 'Italian garden' is still varied and rich, including exotic fuchsias, the tender *Abutilon* and *Cestrum* from Central and South America, camellias, rhododendrons, myrtles and callistemons.

Emerging from the east side of the casita, a huge English lawn stretches all the way to the walled kitchen garden. On Peto's plan this was divided up for croquet and tennis, with flowering shrubs and trees on the north and a heather bank on the south. A border has now been introduced along the northern side of the lawn, planted with a wide range of flowering woody plants – pieris, magnolia, griselinia, acacia, olearia, viburnums, and many more. The path to the east leads through a grand entrance to the walled garden – a Roman arch with a triumphal pediment above and finished with a fine gate of seventeenth-century Spanish wrought-ironwork. On Peto's plan this is called, of course, the kitchen garden (of one-acre). Planned as a necessity for life on the island, it included a range of heated glasshouses on the south-facing wall on either side of a 'flower house', with cold frames spread out in front.

It is apparent that the walled garden is an unusual shape, with no two sides parallel. It is more or less rectangular, but clearly its shape has been determined by expediency to take note of soil and terrain – the shape in the general plan altered in the more detailed drawings. The essential character remained the same, with an indented north wall to provide added shelter for the glasshouses and towers of different design on each of the four main corners. The walls were buttressed all the way round on the outside for strength, but leaving the face of the wall on the inside unencumbered by protrusions, thus being ideal for the training of fruit trees.

The four angular towers on the corners, although all individual, share a common construction of local stone with Bath stone quoins. The tower on the north-west corner was built much taller than the others, taking the form of an Italian *campanile* in the Romanesque

style, with an open belvedere at the top from which to survey the island. There are roundels in the stonework just below the arcaded top level that give the impression that it was intended to include a clock on every face – hence it was called the Clock Tower. The utilitarian need for the garden has disappeared, and now the walled area provides a haven for the plantsman to grow magnificent herbaceous borders, which line the paths that bisect the garden in traditional kitchen garden form.

The other half of the island lying parallel to and south of the formal axis is the complementary Robinsonian wild garden – Bryce's vision of paradise that grows around the long glade of Happy Valley. Peto enjoyed making literary connections and his diaries show his deft use of descriptive language. In his own garden at Iford Manor, he quoted from Tennyson's poem *The Palace of Art*, engraving in the cloister the words 'A haunt of ancient Peace'. At Ilnacullin he was recalling Johnson's *The History of Rasselas*, a story that would have appealed to Peto. It is written as if it were some kind of Arabian tale, with Rasselas, Prince of Abyssinia, tiring of the pleasures of the Happy Valley, escaping in search of real happiness only to discover that it is nowhere to be found. Perhaps the paradox is that happiness really is to be found on this island paradise.

The path follows the natural vale between the rocks, descending from the Martello tower in the east by roughly-hewn steps, crossing a boggy stream at its lowest point, using natural features to emphasise and encourage informal planting. It rises again at the west end and leads out onto a promontory, with a small roofless temple at its furthest point and only the sea and the mountains beyond. It is a symbolic journey through paradise, leaving behind warriors, represented by the fortified tower, to find the gods of Olympus in the temple.

It was intended that the final straight path leading from the steps to the temple on the point of the spur should pass through an avenue of cypresses so that the experience would be like arriving at the mythical temple of the Sibyls at Tivoli – Peto's plan shows a round temple with eight columns as at Tivoli, but what was built was a six-columned, octagonal roofless rotunda. A view of it in an early photograph in the *Observer* in 1935 shows the temple standing out alone on the promontory with the sea below and the mountains behind, conjuring up a scene of a ruined Greek temple in brilliant sunshine high on the cliffs above the Aegean sea.

The trees and shrubs growing along Happy Valley today are a wondrous spectacle for the keen plantsman, with many fine rhododendrons, camellias, pittosporums and the almost unbelievable drooping *Dacrydium cupressinum* from New Zealand, all thriving in the sheltered moist climate of the island. Behind the Happy Valley – effectively the centre of the island that had no name on Peto's plan – is The Jungle, an area of large trees providing shady woodland conditions ideal for the giant tree ferns from New Zealand, the aboreal *Rhododendron falconeri* and the rare *Schima khasiana* from China.

Although a mansion was planned before the First World War, the most active years of work on Ilnacullin between 1911 and 1914 concentrated on buildings for the garden and the planting. Annan

Bryce had decided that the garden must come first. The War intervened, which precluded the possibility of further construction, and after 1918, with the decline of Bryce's financial fortunes, the building of the house was abandoned. The intention had been to crown the highest point of the island, incorporating the existing Martello tower, with a grand Renaissance-style palace planned to have a spectacular tower, a huge entrance loggia, balconies, a semicircular ambulatory on the first floor, and surrounding gardens of balustraded terraces, steps and a belvedere. The great organic-looking structure articulated with bays, recesses and varied roof heights was to be pierced and lightened by balcony window details reminiscent of fifteenth-century Venetian palaces on the Grand Canal or the Palazzo Spanocchi in Siena – palaces which would have been so familiar to Peto.

The detailing of the building and garden is full of antique associations: a Byzantine tomb in the wall of the entrance patio, a Camerino lion as heraldic relief, and then garden statues, vases, columns and a fountain in an octagonal basin. This last is the 'map-paved' privy garden below the old tower, quartered with four mushroom-shaped Portugal laurels to evoke the Old English garden, and then from the corner of the terrace the steps descend on the journey to the Happy Valley. Architectural instructions for the old round tower on the western end give it particular importance: the centre of the music room and the middle of the window must be lined up precisely on the centre of the temple – a piece of alignment which gives substance to the part the Happy Valley plays in uniting the twin destinies – the tower symbolising war and the temple symbolising the gods.

This, wrote Arthur Hellyer in *Country Life* in 1965 is, 'a garden in search of a house' for all the elements of the grand design – the formal garden, tennis and croquet lawns and the walled kitchen garden – are all prerequisites for life in an Edwardian mansion. Yet if the house had been built, the island would be a very different place today. Eden, it is said, had no need for a house. Ilnacullin, the Irish Eden, famous for bringing together two essential aspects of gardening, art and nature, would lose much of its fascination if it had not remained a houseless island.

The bonsai Hinoki Cypress (the golden form of Chamæcyparis obtusa*) was by the pool in early photographs of 1920. Peto introduced similar 'dwarfed' plants to his garden at Iford Manor.*

4:
Villas and Gardens of the Riviera

Isola Bella, Cannes: (above) *The colonnade of the garden house, built on high ground, makes a striking foreground to the distant landscape.*

Villa Rosemary, Cap Ferrat: (left) *This airy open loggia, filled with light and shade, has views over the sparkling sea to Monaco.*

Alongside his practice in England, Peto developed a considerable clientele on the French Riviera where the restrictions in his agreement with his former partnership with Ernest George did not apply. There he was able to give full rein to creating Classical-style villas with the grandeur and yet simplicity of the early Renaissance palaces. He was able to set them in heaven-sent landscapes, often on rocky promontories surrounded by the azure sea, with pergolas on terrace walks and garden pavilions, evoking romantic scenes from Alma-Tadema's paintings. The seaside villas of the Romans are legendary and redolent of the pleasures of life. Their gardens next to the sea, with vantage points and walks, enjoyed much the same views to be found today at, for example, San Michele on Capri, in the gardens created in the early twentieth century by the Swedish physician Axel Munthe, a contemporary of Peto.

As many of Peto's commissions were near Nice on Cap Ferrat, it is difficult to imagine how he supervised his practice at such a distance from England; he must surely have had a local architect acting as his agent during his absence. However, Peto's famous attention to detail,

which can be seen in the photographs of his Riviera villas, shows that he kept very tight control of his projects. The visitors' book at Iford reveals a lack of entries during the winter months, particularly December and January, and one can surmise that this was Peto's preferred time to be away on the Continent managing ongoing work.

It is unclear how his commissions in the South of France came to be initiated, but one of the first approaches was from Ralph Curtis (1854–1922), an expatriate Bostonian, painter and fellow student of John Singer Sargent, and a lifelong friend of Isabella Stewart Gardner (who Peto of course had visited on his trip to America in 1887). Curtis was also a good friend of Henry James; no doubt Peto moved in this circle and so would have been an obvious choice when an architect was needed. Ralph Curtis had married a wealthy young widow, Lisa Rotch, in 1897 (when Ralph was largely living with his parents at the Palazzo Barbaro in Venice), and the idea of a villa on the Riviera was mooted in a letter to Isabella Gardner in April 1901. By February 1902, another letter to Isabella confirms that the Villa Sylvia, named after the Curtises' daughter, was under construction. That same year, Lisa and Ralph visited Peto at Iford. Tipping's article in *Country Life* in 1910 cannot heap enough praises on the Villa Sylvia and its garden, referring to the way its style so perfectly suits its surroundings (in contrast to the failure of other Englishmen to adapt

Villa Sylvia, Cap Ferrat: Peto designed this spacious stairway (left) *to descend from the entrance to the grand saloon on the garden level below.*
(below): *The western façade looks across the garden to the sea, while the back of the house is set against a steep bank.*

to their environment) and how brilliantly the house and garden bring
to mind the villas of Italy.

The Villa Sylvia is situated on a narrow strip of land on the western
edge of Cap Ferrat, overlooking the Villefranche bay to the east of
Nice. Peto astutely grasped the opportunity of positioning the villa at
the top of the site in order to leave most of the land sloping down to
the sea through old olive groves to make a perfectly natural garden.
The house that the Curtises wanted was planned to be modest in the
best of villa traditions, with a wide central three-arched loggia facing
west over the bay, a grand saloon behind, and just two other main
rooms: a dining room at one end and a library at the other. All this
was built against the steep bank, with the bedrooms and other rooms
at road level above. Peto built a palatial staircase to descend from the
entrance to the saloon below. This large room had a richly coffered
ceiling and was furnished in Peto's favoured fifteenth-century Italian
style, featuring a large fireplace of that period with a huge plastered
hood above. From the terrace outside, the loggia steps descended to
the garden, which was left essentially in its natural form and
enhanced with flowery groves among the old olive trees. The formal
area was restricted to the discrete terrace at the side of the house
facing the south loggia; here geometrical beds were profusely planted

and allowed to flower freely to blur the borders' edges, giving a
comfortable transition from rigid lines to natural forms.

Bernard Berenson, the connoisseur of the Renaissance, described
his stay with the Curtises in a letter to Isabella Gardner in February
1911, saying that he was on the Riviera for the first time in his life
and was struck by the beauty of the garden, which he praised as 'a
dream of loveliness. Between Ralph's taste and attention and the
incredible willingness of the soil and climate, floral miracles are
performed here daily.'

Arthur Wilson, the shipping owner from Hull, who had previous
professional dealings with Peto and had probably visited Villa Sylvia,
chose Peto to design and build one of the finest of the Riviera villas:
Maryland, set in a prominent location in the centre of Cap Ferrat.
At Villa Sylvia the building is entered by descending from the road,
whereas at Maryland the reverse is the case: the house is sited above it

Villa Maryland, Cap Ferrat: (above) *One of the finest villas on the Riviera; the gardens have
open vistas to the south, where the ground slopes down a cypress-lined stairway to a fountain
and garden temple. This eye-catching cypress walk* (right), *with immaculately clipped arches, is
a brilliant piece of architectural topiary.*

Overleaf: *This Classical garden house on the western boundary of the site, with steps leading
down to a pool surrounded by Arum lilies, forms an arresting finale to the central garden axis,
which runs the full length of the formal terrace.*

and stairs ascend to garden level through the two-storey cloister. The villa stands proudly on the hill, looking picturesque, and with its different levels, articulated with raised gables and sunny balconies, rising above the arcaded cloisters and open loggias. This spectacular villa was not only featured in *Country Life* in December 1910 (the first of Peto's Riviera villas to appear in its pages), but also in the equivalent French magazine, *La Vie à la Campagne*, in 1910 and 1911.

The site plan shows a substantial villa at one end of a long formal garden, regularly laid out in quarters, and leading to a large parterre in front of the quadrant arms of a pergola to either side of the garden house or temple. The whole appears boat-shaped, with the villa rising on the stern and a long, open deck leading to the temple on the prow. A small lane ran alongside the garden and Peto built a bridge over it to the other half of the garden on sloping ground, with a dominant axial stairway at right angles to the main garden, which led down to another temple.

At the Villa Sylvia, the open loggias help to bring the garden into the villa. The effect is accentuated at Maryland by a large open-arcaded entrance cloister on the south side of the main building leading to the entrance court. This has all the associations of a Roman villa: a large semicircular seat, with the same design as Bridge House in Surrey, Pompeian tables, and bronze bowls on tripod legs. The article in *La Vie à la Campagne* (1911) refers to Maryland as *'Le jardin à l'antique'* and *'le Jardin Romain, qui a le charme prenant et évocateur de quelque fresque d'Herculaneum ou de Pompei'* (The Roman garden which has the compelling and evocative charm of a fresco of Herculaneum or Pompeii). The same article describes the semicircular

Villa Rosemary, Cap Ferrat: (above) *The long terrace falls away gently from the villa towards the south with, to the east, uninterrupted views to the picturesque coastline around Monaco. A pergola on the right is at the foot of the wild hillside above.*

(right): *The upper floors have been carried out into the open with spacious balconies. Along with the two open belvederes on either side, the overall massing of the south front can be usefully compared to the sixteenth-century Villa Medici in Rome.*

pergolas on either side of the temple, with their fluted Grecian Doric columns and their bases painted in Pompeian red. Peto was obviously letting his imagination drift back to those lost seaside villas of the Romans, built in commanding positions like the Emperor Tiberius's villa on the cliffs of Capri, which set the fashion for the Roman villas that once lined the bay of Naples.

At the same time as Peto was designing Maryland, he was working for the Seymour Trowers at Bridge House, and before that at Hartham Park. In all three cases, there are remarkably similar designs for the pools in front of the pavilions or temples with the quadrant pergolas.

This vision of antiquity can also be seen at another of the Cap Ferrat villas, the Villa Rosemary, which was built on the east side of the Cape with views across the bay to Monaco. Peto advised the Englishman Arthur Cohen on the choice of the site, and then built the largest of the Cap Ferrat villas: a palazzo-like, south-facing façade of five bays with projecting wings on either side. The whole building was

on two floors, with squat towers set back at either end – the massing reminiscent of many early Italian palaces, but in particular the Villa Medici at Rome. The ground floor was built with exposed local stone, while the walls above were plastered and, while still wet, scratched to give a diaper patterning in the 'graffito manner'. The terrace on the garden front has projecting loggias on either side and in the middle a central rectangular tank in the style of the Pompeian houses, with a copy of the *amorino* with a fish.

The main garden, which is on this side of the house, was slightly stepped down, making three levelled plats, all taking full advantage of the fine views across the bay to the south and east. A square-columned pergola enclosed the garden on the west side, separating the geometric formality from the wild Robinsonian garden on the hillside above. The focal point at the furthest end from the house was the long, open pavilion of five airy bays with gleaming white arches, which Tipping said was known as the 'Squiffa' (a covered open-sided building) – an idea borrowed from old Moorish gardens – to provide the ideal view back to the villa and here also over the bay to the east.

Peto's letter after the War to Edward James testifies to Peto's popularity on the Cap; his commissions for other villas might well be attributed to his knowledge and clear understanding of the potential of the area. Certainly his reference in this letter to the 'Ephrussi garden' (the Villa Ephrussi de Rothschild) shows that at the very least he advised there, although clearly not very happily since he adds, 'she was too impossible and quarrelsome!' Peto's villa vocabulary invariably includes the use of shady loggias to extend the rooms out into the garden, balconies to let the eye sweep over the sea, the shore and the timeless olive groves, and square towers from which to scan the horizons. Terraced gardens were *de rigueur* and often constructed to give shady walks beneath Amalfi-like pergolas on key vantage points.

Apart from Cap Ferrat, Peto had other inspiring commissions along the Côte d'Azur. Near Cannes in 1910, he worked at the Villa Isola Bella for Baron Van André, creating an entirely new scheme on recently acquired land adjoining the old house and garden. The centrepiece of the design was a large oval pool surrounded by an Ionic colonnade, which recalls the Canopus Canal at Hadrian's Villa. Two monumental gateways, based on the entrance to the Villa Pia at the Vatican, stand at either end of the pool making majestic entrances to the curving colonnades. Steps led down to the water, and the whole conception of this brilliantly lit space and dynamic colonnades reflected in the pool invites comparisons with Peto's other, albeit very different, water gardens at Buscot and Easton, both of them out-standing entities in themselves. The mirror-like pool was built across the slope while another axis rose from below, with the stairway interrupted by the pergola walk around the marble colonnade before ascending the hill to the highest vantage point. Here Peto built

Villa Rosemary, Cap Ferrat: This photograph taken for Country Life *in 1928 from the eastern balcony, some sixteen years after the first series in 1912, demonstrates how the formal layout of the garden has matured and how the growth of the trees at the end now entirely obscured the 'Squiffa'.*

another of his remarkable garden houses. Although the building stands high up on the mound, with its raised central mass surrounded by a projecting open arcade, it is clear that the model was the Charles V pavilion in the Alcázar gardens, Seville (a model which in 1911 Peto also used for the garden house at Ilnacullin). The fountain in the pool is almost like a signature, for Peto was repeating one of his favourites. He chose the bronze *amorino* playing in the coils of the dolphin's tail as the central feature of the pool. It was based on the Greek original (like the key fountain at Buscot), and was positioned here at Isola Bella just at the crossing of the two main axes. It is a great scheme of outstanding simplicity.

Isola Bella, Cannes: This archway (left), photographed c.1911, is seen here in its pristine state shortly after completion, and makes a monumental entrance to the central colonnaded pool. From the centre of the pool (below) a long flight of steps ascends to the garden house just visible at the top. One of Peto's favourite Roman fountains sits in the middle of the pool at the crossing of the two main axes.

At Beaulieu Peto worked for one of the world's most renowned engineers, Gustave Eiffel and his daughter, at the Villa Salles. He had met Eiffel as an engineering contact of his father, Sir Morton, and knew him well enough to be invited to the grand soirées that Eiffel arranged every year in Paris on his birthday. At the Villa Salles (which he did not build), Peto designed one of the most elegant of seaside loggias right on the seafront and close to the villa, which itself stands only a few yards from the shore. Light and airy, it has all the early Renaissance qualities of Brunelleschi's brilliant arcade for the *Ospedale degli Innocenti* (Foundling Hospital in Florence, 1419–44).

Over the years much of the garden has changed, but the photographs that survive are reminiscent of Peto's other imaginative work. At the west end of the garden he designed a semicircular exedra of coupled columns surrounding a Roman bath, with copies of the deer from Herculaneum standing on plinths to either side of the apse, as

they do at Iford Manor. Peto must have maintained his contacts with the Eiffel family after the First World War, as he wrote a letter of condolence to Eiffel's daughter living at Beaulieu on the death of her father in 1923.

*   *   *

Throughout Tipping's *Country Life* articles Peto is the subject of unrestrained admiration for bringing a new spirit to the Riviera gardens. Particularly revealing is the article on Villa Isola Bella which is rightly derisive about the 'Jardin Anglais' of 'endless swelling undulations of turf set wearisomely with every sort of palm, and sprinkled about haphazardly with hard-edged oval beds filled with cinerarias, Chinese primulas and other florists' flowers'. In describing Villa Sylvia, Tipping is at pains to point out Peto's awareness 'of the unity of a house and garden where every part is correlated to every other and where the position and character of every fraction, whether it be roofed or unroofed, are as much part of a definite plan as are the rooms in the house itself.' A sentiment often expressed by the architects of the Arts and Crafts Movement, whose ideas would have been very familiar to Peto. Tipping tells us how Peto links characteristics of nature and of the past, and in this respect, particularly has in mind the gardens of Italy.

Seldom do we know what Peto himself thought of his work but there is a rare glimpse in a letter to Edward James when, now aged seventy-five, Peto looks back over the past. About his commissions on the Riviera he wrote: 'I enjoyed my time there very much, I felt the beauty so much, and introduced a new feeling into building there, which I am glad to think has affected much that is done there now … I did what I felt would have been done in the 15th century, if they had been able, and not harassed by pirates and Saracens, who made all building impossible, except crows nests like Eze.' It is clear from this letter that Peto was full of empathy for the early Renaissance and had strong feelings about the recovery of Classical forms; for him the direct use of artefacts and features from the world of antiquity was an important part of his efforts to reconnect with the Classical world.

Isola Bella, Cannes: (left) *A breathtaking vision of the long Ionic colonnade, pergola, curving pool, fountain and archway, all bound together in a single composition.*

Villa Salles, Beaulieu: (overleaf) *Unlike the villas on Cap Ferrat, which were high up on the peninsula, this villa is right next to the sea. The architecturally simple, lofty colonnades are unmistakeably designed by Peto, but it is rare to see his work without the embellishment of an abundance of flowering climbers.*

5:
Iford Manor:
A Garden
at Last

When Harold Peto left his partnership with Ernest George in 1892 to search for a place in the country, his motivation, as so often expressed in his diaries, particularly during his trip to Greece in 1891, was to leave London and make a garden. This search for his 'ideal of a country house', often made with his friend Avray Tipping, and recounted twenty years later in *The Boke of Iford*, had lasted for most of the decade. During that time, after a brief stay at Hernden in Kent, he had moved to Landford House, Salisbury, and while there discovered Iford Manor, which he 'felt at once realised more than could be hoped of all my dreams'. But according to his friend Tipping, Peto had known that the house was on the market for at least a year and had expressed his misgivings about the fact that the garden lay behind and above the house, while the front was closed off by the road and river. Peto also recalled that it was a much larger house and estate than he was looking for, but finally the charm of Iford's position won him over and he managed to complete the purchase in 1899 with, it is said, the help of his sister Helen.

The house sits next to the River Frome at the bottom of the valley, with the ground rising sharply up behind the buildings and a hanging

wood above spreading on to the brow of the hill. The front of the main house facing onto the river has an eighteenth-century façade, about 1730, with, as Peto thought at first, the remains of a slightly earlier house behind. However, in the course of initial renovations he was jubilant to discover an earlier stone-mullioned window of four lights dating back to the fifteenth century. He set about removing more modern partitions to regain the spaces of the much earlier Tudor dwelling, but after these discoveries and necessary repairs he immediately directed his attention to the garden. The steep hillside demanded terraces and steps, and retaining walls, quite unlike the landscape and surroundings of most of his future commissions. For Peto comparisons with the hillside gardens of Italy, around Rome, Tuscany and the Lakes, must have been obvious. He talks in *The Boke* of the importance of structure as opposed to 'masses of colour irrespective of form', and he saw instantly the opportunities that the sloping ground gave him. But progress was slow, almost organic, taking many years, so it was not until 1914 that the garden was more or less complete.

The Garden Gate

The relationship of house to garden in this situation was of key importance – the central front door of the eighteenth-century south-facing elevation opened onto the forecourt where, due to the lane in front, enlargement was impossible. There was no entrance to the upper garden except by a path that trailed round the south-east corner of the house and up the slope. In addition, Peto had to contend with

Above: Peto generally collected authentic pieces of sculpture that came from the hand of the sculptor. However, when that was impossible he chose the best copy he could afford – in this case, a bronze cast of the Dying Gaul, *mounted over the gateway to the kitchen garden and clearly in view from the loggia balcony.*

Left: This eighteenth-century elevation, delightfully clothed in wisteria and climbing roses, conceals a much earlier Tudor house, which Peto began to uncover in the course of renovations after his arrival in 1899.

an extension at this end, a sham wing above, which virtually blocked access to the main garden and hid the view of the bridge from the upper garden. He immediately demolished the sham façade and extension, and in their place built the three-arched loggia with graceful Ionic columns and a flat roof above, which was accessible from the main bedroom floor of the house. To enhance the garden entrance was vital. To achieve this Peto built, from the corner of the house to the boundary, a dividing wall pierced by a simple Pompeian doorway, with a niche above, giving access to the Fountain Court that he created in front of the loggia. This innovation made a significant transition from the forecourt to the secluded and sheltered sitting area in front of the loggia commanding a view up the great stairway, ascending to the terraces. A large wisteria was already established at the corner of the house when Peto first came; cleverly (and characteristically) he gave it a special round window in the dividing wall so that its progress was not impeded. The courtyard entrance outside the loggia was planted with irises and then dramatically staged, with two large plinths supporting copies of the bronze deer from Herculaneum; while between them the semicircular pool, with a lion's mask fountain in the wall, freshened the air with its steady stream. Seen from inside, the loggia arcade forms the proscenium arch to a stage in the form of the rectangular court and apse, with the steps and the garden gate providing exits on either side.

A Stairway to the Terraces and Beyond
Very early photographs of Iford show a rough flight of steps, in the same position as they are today, ascending the slope to the higher terraces with dry stone retaining walls on either side – they were undoubtedly there when Peto arrived. The initiation for change and development is to be found in his visitors' book, where an early entry by the garden writer and friend Inigo Triggs in June 1900 includes a drawing of the steps at an Elizabethan house near Bath, with the words, 'In remembrance of a busy day at St Catherine's Court'.

Above: *Elegant piers form a dramatic entrance to the stairway, which ascends the garden in the direction of the great terrace.*

Right: *The Fountain Court. The copies of bronze deer from Herculaneum are perfectly framed in the proscenium arches of the loggia.*

Triggs and Peto had visited the garden together and no doubt Triggs was busy measuring and drawing it; the similarities of the situation at Iford are obvious: St Catherine's was also built at the foot of a slope and the axial flight of steps leads from the side to the higher terraces. The triple stairway at Iford was already a godsend for Peto, but with his talents he further developed the stages of the ascent by adding ashlar Bath stone pillars butted against the retaining walls to either side; these are already in evidence by the time of the first *Country Life* article in 1907. Later, he continued to refine the walls by adding edge moulded copings so that the view up the stairway was dramatically formalised from terrace to terrace. Of course, structure, as he tells us, was important to him, but so also was planting. The coping stones on the walls have round holes cut at intervals to carry pots or plants, and photographs of the steps show that foliage was encouraged to grow freely in the crevices.

The Great Terrace

After ascending the stairway and crossing the upper lawn, the main terrace was reached by a scramble up a grassy bank. Peto tells us that 'The Terrace, being the main feature of the Garden, came in for a predominating share of what I was proposing to do.' One of the first things Peto did before he began work on the terrace itself, was to drastically thin the overgrown hanging woods above. In his article in *Country Life* in 1907, Tipping described the success of these changes: 'the clean stems ... the glint of sun through the foliage, the aspect of the horizon through the glades'. Peto had inherited the long grassy terrace (perhaps his vision for it had been a deciding factor in the purchase of Iford), which had been there for at least a century, as it is recalled in *Country Life* that Thomas Gaisford, Dean of Christ Church, Oxford, and owner of Iford in the early nineteenth century, described the terrace as 'the most classic thing he knew, a congenial and inspiring spot when engaged on his literary labours'. At the west end overlooking the orchard, the previous owner, Captain Rooke had placed Ionic capitals (from the old house which once stood in what is now the kitchen garden) and the family crest of a rook on a wheat sheaf on two pillars on either side of the terrace, as if to make an entrance but instead he blocked off the end of the terrace between the piers with iron railings. At the other end there was no feature – the terrace losing itself aimlessly in bushes and a grassy bank.

One of Peto's first decisive acts was to remove 'a charming little George II Garden House from a mount in the Kitchen Garden' and rebuild it, replacing thatch with stone tiles, at the east end – thus the terrace was closed off at both ends. At the same time as the reconstruction of the garden house, which he describes as having 'a panelled Dado, and Door, Windows & Fireplace ... *c*.1720', Peto built steps at this point to descend from the terrace using a balustrade, which he had rescued from the river. Early photographs show that he lined the grassy terrace with all kinds of pots, tubs with trees, shrubs

Previous pages: *The upper floors of the house look out over the terraces and a great assemblage of planting at the centre of this magnificent hillside garden.*

Left: *The articulated colonnade and flights of steps emphasise this staged entrance to the great terrace. Views through and beyond were always in Peto's mind.*

and even bonsai trees, interspersed with a few busts on pedestals, and at the west end a wellhead in front of the railing fence. Already the terrace has the making of a ceremonial progress, a triumphal way in the Roman manner, between Peto's cherished features that he was to augment over the years. He had to make two important structural decisions to achieve this vision.

Once on the terrace, Peto needed to enhance the vista and he chose to pave the entire length with coursed York stone, the jointing of which gave the desired perspective; he made the paved way somewhat narrower than the width of the terrace, ensuring that he could have a broad border of gravel on either side on which to arrange his potted plants and sculptures. He replaced the bank with a retaining wall, and below the terrace he used the old lily pool as the pivotal point from which to construct a double stairway to either side, 'round the great Portugal Laurel', and thus replace the slippery bank. This assured that ascent to the terrace was dignified but easy. At this time, in about 1903, there were no colonnades and no balustrades overlooking the lily pool, no staircase ascending to the hill above the terrace and no additions to the west end. Where the casita is today there was an old rustic tool shed, and on the lower side an old lean-to greenhouse against the west wall.

Peto tells us he placed Classical stone columns around the lily pool, linked together by a wooden architrave on which he grew wisteria. Although colonnades around pools were not something he developed elsewhere – usually balustrades were preferred, although Isola Bella is an exception – there were precedents with which he would have been familiar. His collection of ephemera at Dumbarton Oaks in Washington includes a postcard of the pool at the Parc Monceau in Paris, an eighteenth-century folly of a ruined colonnade surrounding a large water basin. The idea could easily be derived from the surviving ruins at Hadrian's villa. Both of them might have inspired Peto's simple embellishment of the pool at Iford. The colonnade collapsed after the Second World War and was removed.

Roman Seats

In trying to unravel the sequence of garden-making, the *Country Life* photographs of 1907 give a clear picture of what was achieved by that

Above: *Peto saw the colonnade as an essential adjunct to the line of the great terrace. Here at the west end, the columns on either side are used to concentrate the vista, and also at this point to frame the most delightful of his many garden houses, the casita.*

Right: *At the top of the main stairway a glance back and down over the valley reveals again how careful Peto was to combine shrubs and trees to complement the structural lines of walls and terraces.*

date. It had been necessary to remove the ugly iron fence at the west end of the terrace and close the vista. To accomplish this Peto constructed a semicircular stone seat that in *The Boke* he described as 'apse like' and 'rather on the lines of a basilica'; this analogy suggests that the great terrace itself became the aisle and the wellhead in front of the seat became the font. The notion of the base plan of a basilica had already surfaced as a possible motif for the space in front of the loggia in the Fountain Court. Aesthetically, the seat provides both a rounding off and a closure to the direction of the terrace – a comforting finality – and at the same time leaves the space through the pillars open to view the orchard that drops away immediately behind.

These semicircular stone seats were to become a popular feature and were included in many of Peto's subsequent commissions. Their underlying symbolism conceals an alternative interpretation for the terrace: at Pompeii the semicircular seats on the Street of the Tombs were in remembrance of distinguished Roman citizens, and marked the place of the burial of their ashes. With this in mind, the Roman and Greek sarcophagi displayed along the great terrace become a reference to the notion of the Roman or Appian Way, which commemorated great lives.

Peto was very conscious of these Roman seats. He kept a photograph of the priestess Mamia's exedra at Pompeii, now in the Dumbarton Oaks collection, and was also familiar with the use of such seats in Alma-Tadema's paintings. The paintings enabled him to copy the architectural detail for the seat ends, which he used in other designs, for example at Hartham and Buscot. At Iford he chose to keep the seats simple, without sculpted ends, although the idea of placing small columns in preference to more elaborate seat ends might well have come from the Alinari photograph of Pompeii he owned. This shows the second of the two seats with just such a configuration. In his travel diaries, whenever he comes across a semicircular seat, Peto refers to it as a 'Tadema' seat. The *Country Life* photograph of 1907 reinforces this vision of the Roman world: a copy of a bronze Pompeian tripod table is on view at the focal point. All the work of restructuring the end of the terrace was done before the removal of the glasshouse that was on the lower side and the tool shed above.

The Colonnades

Peto's next ambitious move, soon after 1907, was to give a stronger presence to the terrace and further develop its Classical associations. Above the lily pool, where he had already constructed the double stairway to the terrace, he built a short, monumental Ionic colonnade, returned at either end, to embrace both flights of steps. To balance this he decided to erect a double Tuscan colonnade with stone architrave, on either side of the west end, to dramatise the star-studded approach to the circular seat; the terrace at its mid-point was already partially confined by the steepness of the hillside above the double staircase. The colonnade on the lower side restricted visual alignment to the terrace walk, but at the same time made windows through

The crossing point on the great terrace, with steps leading up the hill to the King Edward VII column or down to the oval lily pool. The colonnade, on the right, and the oil jars, on the left, lead the eye to the George II garden house that closes the vista.

which to view the lower garden and the valley beyond – that illusion of a Tuscan hillside.

Along the terrace between the colonnades, Peto continued the theme of a Roman or Pompeian street by placing single columns at intervals, and by looping chains between them, enclosing the terrace with flowery curtains or garlands of roses and clematis. Many of the columns in the garden are antique pieces that Peto procured on his travels, but in the case of the terrace all the columns were made from local stone from the Westwood quarries.

The Collector

Over the years some of his most unusual acquisitions found their way on to the terrace. Among them two marble sarcophagi, the one Greek and the other Roman, a seventeenth-century Italian figure of a philosopher, a marble female bust from the time of Louis XIV, a bench supported on two fourteenth-century Venetian capitals, a wellhead made from one of Theodric's Byzantine capitals discovered in Bologna and two great oil jars – Peto said they were from Nice and the 'largest

Above: The double flight of steps can be seen rising beneath the colonnade onto the great terrace, and then single columns direct the eye in the direction of the garden house.

Left: From the great terrace the colonnade steps descend to either side of the lily pool, which is set almost in the centre of the garden. This photograph reinforces the view that the middle of the slope has been deliberately kept open with more natural planting.

I have ever seen' – opposite the double stairway and at the foot of the stairs to the Edward VII column.

That Harold Peto was a collector is without doubt – he cherished objects for their associations as he did buildings. He said in *The Boke* that 'fragments of Masonry carry one's mind back to the past in a way that a garden entirely of flowers cannot do', and later, 'These bits of old sculpture I feel are so much more as the Artist left them, than is the case with pictures.' In his youth when he was in Venice in 1888, he wrote, 'I don't and won't care how worn my clothes are on the busses I ride on if only I can get beautiful things to live with.' All his life, he was in constant touch with dealers and regularly received photographs of pieces that were for sale. He was on the look out for gems for himself and for his clients, one of whom was Isabella Gardner, who built Fenway Court, the Italian palace in Boston, and when he designed gardens he frequently included spaces for statues, fountains or architectural features – he saw them as an integral part of landscape design. He was once sent a postcard of the Vicenza Giardino dalle Ore Quirini, showing the principal avenue lined with sculptures all the way down; he kept this card among his ephemera presumably because he liked the idea of it.

Peto was not a collector in the sense that he wanted to make a museum – museum collections were of little interest to him, as will be

seen when he was deciding on the form of the cloister. Comparisons between Iford and Peto's other garden designs reveal that the collection of objects at Iford played an important part in this design but, significantly, his other garden commissions without exception relied in the first place on the structural and architectural spaces and the planting, and not on assembled sculpture.

Together with his desire to make a landscape of memories, rather than memorials, Peto had an equal passion for plants: scrutiny of the photographs of Iford shows that he grew climbers in profusion to embellish the many architectural features. In particular, the record shows that along the terrace, the columns, chains and architraves were 'moderately clothed', as Gertrude Jekyll would say, rather than suffering from an 'overgrowth', and articles describe garlands of roses and clematis. Campanulas and other species had been encouraged to colonise the steps and paving stones.

Garden Rooms

The great terrace, as it is now called, probably more than any other part of the garden, continued to be developed right up to the First World War. The addition of the colonnade at the west end had

necessitated the demolition of the old greenhouse, which was left over from the old kitchen garden that had previously been located on this site. (The new walled kitchen garden, which Peto used, was on the other side of the road further east along the riverbank). In its place, he built the first of the 'garden rooms' or courts that run down the western wall of the slope. They are connected by a series of steps that make an alternative route to the terrace. The little court at the top, about which he speaks in *The Boke*, is centred around a small shallow basin made with blue mosaic, and in the wall above he built in some of his most precious pieces; he draws attention to 'a woman riding on a tiger', saying how unusual it was, dating from pre-Byzantine times. This is known as 'Tempi Bassi'. The small pool, with its moulded surround, is reminiscent of the shallow Roman basins found in many of the houses at Pompeii, and often depicted in Alma-Tadema's paintings.

Above: *The wellhead, the column and the semicircular Roman seat form the culmination to the western end of the great terrace. Beyond, between the square columns (from the previous garden), there is a glimpse of the orchard.*

Right: *The rounded shapes of clipped phillyreas frame a compelling view past the wellhead and the column to the central point: the Pompeian tripod and bowl, seen here between the double Verona marble columns of the casita.*

The Casita

The photographs in the *Architectural Review*, 1913, of the area above the west end of the terrace show mature planting and a wisteria growing well over the architrave of the colonnade. However, behind it, the stone-tiled old tool shed is still in place. Although conceivably this photograph may have been taken some time before its publication, it is clear that the building of the 'Casita'– as this loggia was always referred to by Peto – was a late event, perhaps begun in 1912. This is one of his most endearing buildings; perfectly sited and constructed with its back to the hill and open views to the front through the colonnade and over the terrace, and yet perfectly secluded in the top-most north-west corner of the garden. It is, by other names a loggia or pavilion, long and narrow, with a shallow-pitched roof, hipped at either end – not unlike the roof of the pavilions at Ilnacullin and Bridge House. It is stone-tiled in a local vernacular style but, that said, other aspects of its construction are borrowed mainly from Italy, although Tipping, referring to the casita in 1922, called it 'a Spanish form of loggia'. The *Boke* says it is the structure 'into which I built many of my pieces of old Italian marble', which

included the small wheel window carved in stone, '14th century Venetian'.

The casita is made with three bays, as in the pavilions of his other gardens but, in this case, pairs of slender pink Verona marble columns, 'dating from about 1200', divide them and support a highly decorative architrave, probably of Venetian origin. The casita is extended to either side beyond the bays to form enclosed wings, but one of its great advantages is that it is shallow, which allows it to be filled with sunlight and warmth. So often open loggias like this are designed much too deep with the result that they are damp and musty through lack of air. To build the casita, Peto used old weathered stone that he obtained from pulling down old barns and pigsties. Inside, he built a simple central niche into the middle of the back wall. The whole building makes the most perfect setting for contemplation.

One other feature immediately arising from the great terrace is the staircase, which continued up the steep bank opposite the lily pool bringing the hanger, or 'hanging wood' as it is called, into the garden area. The lower part is contained within a low parapet wall that is 'ramped' up at intervals in the same way as the design for the Buscot steps. At the top, Peto placed a column supporting a Roman capital and a figure of the infant Zeus, all dedicated to the memory of Edward VII. It was not inscribed until the middle of the First World War,

Left: *A distant view of the cloister behind tall lime trees at the eastern end of the garden.*
Below: *A stepping-stone approach to the cloister, both rich in detail but simple overall, was the last major architectural work at Iford, completed around 1914.*

following a visit from the then Speaker of the House of Commons, J. W. Lowther, who wrote the dedication 'To King Edward VII the peacemaker', which Peto immediately had inscribed on the column. In 1916, with carnage going on at the front, it seems somewhat ironic to refer back to the efforts of Edward VII to develop the *entente* in Europe (his influence is now disputed by recent historians).

The Cloister

The last major building, and easily the largest in terms of the scale of work at Iford, was the construction of the cloister. The *Country Life* article published early in 1913, makes no mention of it but it is likely that work began later that year as the project was well advanced by the end of 1914. Peto had been pleased with the success of the casita and this had encouraged him to design a larger building to contain his now considerable collection of what he called his 'Antique fragments'. Avray Tipping in *Country Life*, 1922, in referring to the cloister and its collection, digresses on the dangers of creating a museum atmosphere: 'Nothing', he says, 'is more contrary to the aesthetic charm of the personal domicile than the museum spirit.' For him the museum is about specimens 'collected in order to yield information' and 'Serried ranks of scheduled items are entirely right' for this. He declares that Peto is not a collector in the sense that he wants to make a museum and that his skill at placing objects avoids any 'suspicion of the museum atmosphere'. The decision to build a cloister to house the fruits of his many years of collecting suggests a very different approach to these fragments of history.

Peto liked the idea of the cloister as a building – one that gave seclusion, one that was not inside or out – for he liked the openness to the sky at its centre, but also the sense of being inside and protected from the world outside. It was for these reasons that the cloister form developed as a place for spiritual contemplation: it provided an atmosphere devoid of worldly distractions, and yet the spirit was free. On his travels to Sicily in 1895, Peto had been fascinated by the monastery cloisters at Monreale, just outside Palermo, where he referred to the 'coupled marble columns with most delicately carved caps', which may twenty years later have helped in his choice of 'Italian Romanesque *c*.1200'. He actually chose a very simple arcaded structure for the cloister at Iford, using Pavonazzo marble for the twin columns from the South of France, and 'the caps and bases are of Istrian stone and were worked in Venice'. These little descriptions of details, taken from *The Boke,* give an enormous insight into his fastidious attention to detail. This was evident in his approaches to all his commissions, as for example the few surviving letters to William James quoted in the earlier chapter on West Dean (see page 41).

All that is to be seen on approaching the cloister, with its low-pitched, stone-tiled roof, are the sturdy walls decorated with relief sculptures, and just two arcaded window openings, in what appears to be a two-storey building with a fine entrance doorway in the centre –

Right: *The double columns around the ambulatory of the cloister could well have been inspired by Peto's visit in 1895 to the twelfth-century cloister at Monreale outside Palermo, Sicily.*

Overleaf: *A small courtyard, with wall fountain, statues and Classical fragments, has echoes of the atrium of a Roman house.*

'from a house in Mantua *c*.1450', *The Boke* tells us. This was all by design, for Peto had been particularly impressed, during his visit to Granada in 1888, that many of the buildings from the Islamic period gave no indication on the outside of what was contained within. He used this simple principle in many aspects of his garden design, where discreet planning enabled the revelation of fresh views at all times, as the direction taken unfolded. It is like this once in the cloister: walking around, there are always new views and new pieces to be encountered.

Inside the cloister, above the arch to the central garth, is inscribed the words 'A Haunt of Ancient Peace', a line from Tennyson's poem *The Palace of Art*; these words might be seen as both appropriate and prophetic, for the poem describes a person, perhaps not unlike Peto, who devoted a life to collecting art to adorn a sumptuous palace. Eventually, tired and wretched, the collector of these treasures desires nothing more than an English home: 'On dewy pastures, dewy trees, Softer than sleep – all things in order stored, A haunt of ancient Peace'. This phrase in particular charmed many Edwardian minds, and John Dando Sedding in his book *Garden-Craft* (1892) eulogises the concept of a garden with 'that air of inviting mystery and homely reserve that our forefather loved … an old English garden "a haunt of ancient peace".' It was an idea that became synonymous with the Old English garden; it was a dream that in the new world, the post nineteenth-century industrial world, a longed-for peace could be found. Iford Manor had lived up to that ideal for Tipping. In his article of 1907, he quotes the phrase from Tennyson and describes the Manor in its 'happy valley of rural England' where the 'Arcadian silence is seldom broken by the motor's hoot, for its narrow, rough and precipitous lanes fitly keep the rapid wayfarer to the high road far away on the hill.'

Rills, Stepping Stones and Memories of Japan

Among all the dominating and attention-seeking features it is easy to overlook the natural-looking areas, which Peto planned with just as much art and detailed attention. These were begun very early on in the development of the garden, for he says in *The Boke*, 'I laid on the water from the beautiful springs in the wood which enabled me to have a modest arrangement of fountains and a small runnel of water through the rock garden.' After leaving the cloister in the direction of the house, the path crosses the centre of the slope through a space of shrubs and rocks where the stones have been laid with great care – in one place to make a little rill for the stream, and in another to provide a way over the water, with stepping stones which are so carefully worked together that nothing can be more reminiscent of the Japanese art of placing stones. Apart from this, there is no mention in *The Boke* of making a Japanese garden. However, there was an area above the great terrace where there was evidence of Peto's interest – a natural

pool fed by a spring, and Japanese lanterns placed discreetly on the banks. His experiences in Japan had left a firm impression and he wanted to hold on to memories of that trip, which for him included an appreciation of what he saw as gardens of the 'natural garden type', and also of the 'miniaturised' or bonsai plants which he imported from Japan and sometimes sold to his clients, as in the case of Annan Bryce at Ilnacullin.

Sense of Place

Overall, the plan of Iford reflects nothing of the schemes Peto used for his major commissions. Broadly speaking, all the incidents – the small garden rooms at the western end, the terrace and casita and the cloister – are all on the edges of the main garden. It is as if the axis of the triple stairway arrives at the centre that is open, with lawns and shrubs, whereas around the periphery there are Classical colonnades and buildings. Peto has subverted the notion of progression from the artificial to the natural – very different from commissions like Heale or Buscot, where the formal structures extend out into the natural landscape, or Easton where the formal arena gives way to the 'bosquet' and the 'wild garden'. This was not necessarily a conscious decision, but rather a sensitive response to his environment: to work with it rather than dominate it, and not to disregard the natural topography. For all the garden's borrowings from Classical times, Iford remains, with its 'sense of place', an essentially English garden, more so than the large, formal commissions like Crichel and Buscot. With its open centre of sloping lawns and shrubs and its surrounding cycle of features, it is an odyssey, comparable to Stourhead on a small scale. It is a Classical journey through an English landscape.

For all Peto's journeyings abroad and his borrowings there is a nationalistic pride in his landscape vision. The Edward VII column is an obvious manifestation of his feelings, as is the statue of Britannia that he erected around 1910 on the bridge parapet over the river, just outside the main gates (it appears in a small watercolour in his visitors' book in May 1911). On Empire day (the birthday of Queen Victoria on 24 May), he invited local schoolchildren to take part in

Left: Soon after Peto arrived at Iford, he built this east-facing loggia to make the all-important transition from house to garden.

Right: A fifteenth-century style chimney hood in the garden hall is complemented by early oak furniture, reminiscent of the interior decoration of Peto's London house in Collingham Gardens, and the Riviera villas.

celebrations at Iford and to march past the figure of Britannia draped in the Union Jack. On a different note he also felt the desire to make a spiritual connection to Iford. After building the cloister, which he always saw as containing the spiritual life for which these kinds of buildings were originally intended, he had it dedicated with a Mass in August 1916.

It could be just the wheel of Fortune which determines whether a garden creation survives. If so fate has been very generous to Iford, thanks to the family who inherited the Manor and their enlightened decision to sell it to the present owners, who have become the trusted guardians of this garden, which is an outstanding epitaph to a man of such talent. Not only have the monumental features been conserved and restored, but the living landscape has continued to grow and enhance the garden that Peto left behind in 1933. Below the great terrace a fine example of *Cercidiphyllum Japonicum* continues to mature – an early planting which must be more or less coeval with the one at Heale House. Near the semicircular seat, topiary phillyreas, one of Peto's favourites from the Mediterranean, still frame the view along the terrace. The mature hanging wood on the hillside has been thinned again to restore light to the Japanese maples, *Acer palmatum,* which are highly appreciated for their fresh green foliage in the spring. The enormous plane tree at the foot of the steps to the Edward VII column, there at least since the time of Dean Gaisford, still grows to spread its dappled shade over the centre of the great terrace. The Martagon lilies remain naturalised in the long grass on the approach to the cloister, and the Japanese cherry that was one of Peto's introductions has been replanted from cuttings after the original tree died; now the eponymous cherry, the Iford Cherry, thrives once again. Few gardens can have been so fortunate as Iford and it is a fortune that is highly deserved.

Open informal planting is at the core of the garden, with distant views giving just a glimpse of the colonnade – a reminder of the many architectural features that surround its centre.

The Test
of Time

Iford Manor, Wiltshire: (above) *An early photograph of the kitchen garden.*
(right): *The great terrace.*

Many of Peto's commissions were carried out over several years, as is the nature of gardens and planting, and were often added to in phases, as at Buscot Park and Bridge House. The period from 1900 to the War was a very active one for him, with projects underway simultaneously in England, Ireland and in France. He was just sixty when hostilities broke out in 1914, and planting for such important gardens as Ilnacullin was at a critical stage. The War came at a peak time for him, and his years of active design were consequently curtailed Did he have the heart to create again after the War was ended? It was a very different world – economically and socially there had been seismic shifts – and both people and things he cared about had been destroyed.

He was keenly aware of this destruction and loss. Writing in *The Boke,* he refers to one of his most precious objects, the seated Virgin and Child in the cloister, and remarks: 'I heard after I had bought this figure that it came from the man who was Clerk of Works at the "restoration" of Rheims Cathedral some years ago, and I think it very probable he stole it from there, which is perhaps some consolation to think it has been saved from the awful Holocaust that has taken place in this war, as a large part of the sculpture has been wrecked and burnt.'

Today, contemporary writers on Edwardian gardens seek to characterise Peto's work as Italian in style and largely formal, with an over-emphasis on sculpture. Clearly his diaries, *The Boke*, and his admission to Edward James of the importance of the early Italian Renaissance show that Italy played a key role in the inspiration of his garden design. However, a close look at many of his varied compositions and the detailing of specific features also reveals the influence of his other travels abroad, particularly to France, Spain and Japan. These other influences undermine the simplistic view that his use of Classical features fits a narrow definition of what is loosely called Italian. A closer look at the way he used these elements shows that his vision was coloured by a notion of the recovery of the past – that lost Aegean world upon which the Renaissance was based.

His very individual responses to commissions showed his tendency to respond to a sense of place – the hillside at Iford and the surroundings of Heale House are topographically so different that they called for a very different garden experience. Such sites in less sensitive hands than Peto's would not have achieved such a perfect synthesis between landscape and art. Appreciation of the significance of water in the garden was a *sine qua non* in his response to place. He constructed small tanks and runnels at Iford, large balustraded pools at Easton Lodge and tranquil canals at Bridge House. His *pièce de resistance* was the chain of pools, steps and rills composing the central axis of the inspired Water Garden at Buscot Park. These varied approaches all stem from the diverse cultural influences of Italy, Japan and Islam.

Garden houses and pavilions are another prominent feature of Peto's larger designed landscapes: the pavilions at Hartham and Bridge House deriving from Italian models, whereas the garden houses at Ilnacullin and Isola Bella are taken from the building in the Spanish gardens in Seville. The casita at Iford is an intriguing blend of diverse elements: a roof made from English stone tiles, columns from Verona, a wheel window from Venice and another from Germany, yet overall it draws its inspiration from Spain. The cloister, too, at Iford owes as much to Peto's experience of Islamic architecture as it does to Romanesque Italian.

Iford is sometimes spoken of as being a sculpture gallery, and comparisons have been made with Lord Astor's collection at Hever Castle. Undoubtedly, Peto was a prodigious and discerning collector of those objects which 'carry one's mind back', but as Tipping was careful to stress in his *Country Life* article, Peto did not have a 'museum' attitude to his collecting: he chose pieces that people in the past had made and cherished and thought beautiful. Nor did he display his collection in any sense as a gallery. For him the odyssey of the garden path was one of discovery, and the sculpture placed there helped to create a new vision of the past – this is an aspect of his work much admired by the late garden-maker and poet Ian Hamilton Finlay. Apart from Iford, Peto's garden commissions seldom reflect a large reliance on sculpture – strategic pieces are placed to articulate the composition and seats and fountains are focal points, yet there is never a large accumulation of sculpture.

Of course, Peto has been used as a scapegoat by all those horticultural garden writers, like William Robinson, who say that architects should never design gardens because they know nothing about plants. Inevitably, when assessing the work of an Edwardian garden designer, we are left with the hard landscaping when many of the plants have long gone. A case has sometimes been made for Peto's success as a plantsman, and a few twentieth-century garden writers have appreciated his planting talents. Miles Hadfield wrote in 1966: 'What differentiated Peto from such architects as Robinson's arch enemy, Blomfield … was that Peto understood a great deal about plants and, one now feels, was able to use trees and shrubs, the structural elements in garden design, more effectively than Robinson or Miss Jekyll.' But when it comes to this aspect of his work the photographs have to speak for themselves. The hard landscaping and the structures were of course crucially important to him, but scrutiny of contemporary photographs of his gardens shows how much he relied on dressing those structures to present the plants in their glory. The details in his Japanese diary in particular show that he was having a 'love affair' with plants that would be the benchmark for all his future designs.

Curiously, in his early diaries, although constantly expressing his delight in flowers, Peto never wrote of his need for a garden. Rather, in his youthful excitement in Florence in the 1880s, there is constant enthusiasm for the discovery of paintings and sculpture, and much less mention of architecture and landscape. It is not until the 1890s that he yearns to make a garden, and it is this impulse that drove him to leave London and his architectural partnership. Even by 1896, when gardening had become his passion (and would remain so), he could write while in Venice: 'It is a ceaseless wonder to me that I, as enthusiastic a gardener as lives, can be so perfectly content in this one place in the world where gardening is almost an impossibility.'

Apart from the admiration that Gertrude Jekyll expressed for his work and the frequent accolades heaped on him by Avray Tipping in his *Country Life* articles, Peto's contemporaries recorded very little assessment of his work. Nor indeed is there any record of what Peto thought of the new works of garden design that he saw around him; Lutyens, Mawson and Inigo Thomas were all key players in the Edwardian era, about whom Peto would have had opinions, but it is tantalising that none of his views have survived. *The Boke* contains only generalisations and the occasional aside, which provide only an inkling of his keenly felt distastes – the strongest criticism being reserved for English gardens that are made 'without the slightest attempt at form … and all the most discordant colours huddled together'.

Peto manifestly thought deeply about his own work and the historical gardens that he visited. Throughout this overview of his major designs, *The Boke of Iford* has been a consistent source of evidence for the direction he was taking and the principles moulding his decisions, but there are few gleanings to be found of his personal view of his own commissions. *The Boke* for him served as a way of presenting a 'life work', not so much as a coherent narrative, but as a series of incidents and collected historical artefacts on which to reflect. Most revealing of all is the short quotation from Voltaire that he chose to write on the flyleaf of the bound manuscript of *The Boke*: '*Le mieux est l'ennemi du bien*', (The best is the enemy of the good). These words suggest that for Peto, acting on immediate inspiration brought the best results – revision and reworking would only detract from the initial vision. (If, for instance, the story about the 'birth' of the design for Ilnacullin is true then the plan was laid down right away, without any apparent deviations.)

Peto's perceptions were both sophisticated and complex – the bold but elaborate layouts, the clear and immediate understanding of the scope of each project, the variety and the range of influences – but ultimately, the sources of his vision lay in simple, enduring forms as this visual record of his outstanding gardens powerfully demonstrates.

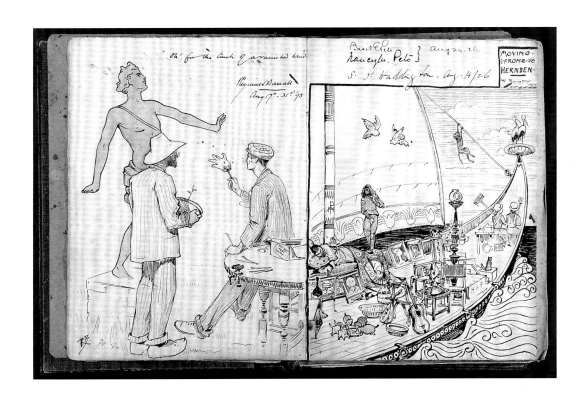

Peto's visitors' book is full of illustrations recording significant moments in his life.
Here, on the right, Peto's move from Hernden to Landford in 1895–96
is depicted by Reginald Barratt.

BIBLIOGRAPHY

Ackerman, James S., *The Villa: Form and Ideology of Country Homes*, Thames & Hudson, 1990.

Airs, Malcolm, editor, *The Edwardian Great House*, Oxford University, 2000.

Aslet, Clive: *The Last Country Houses*, Yale University Press, London, 1982.

Bisgrove, Richard, *The Gardens of Gertrude Jekyll*, Frances Lincoln, London, 1992.

Bowe, Patrick, *Gardens of the Roman World*, Frances Lincoln, 2004.

Bradley-Hole, Kathryn, *Lost Gardens of England: From the Archives of Country Life*, Aurum Press, London, 2004.

—, *Villa Gardens of the Mediterranean*, Aurum Press, London, 2006.

Brooks, Edward C., *Sir Samuel Morton Peto*, Bury Clerical Society, Bury St Edmunds, 1996.

Brown, Jane, *Eminent Gardeners*, Viking, London, 1990.

—, *The English Garden Through the Twentieth Century*, Garden Art Press, Woodbridge, 1999.

Cane, Percy, *Modern Gardens, British and Foreign*, The Studio, London, 1926.

Colonna, Francesco, *Hyperotomachia Poliphili: The Strife of Love in a Dream*, (translation), with an introduction by Joscelyn Godwin, Thames & Hudson, London, 1999.

Cooper, Nicholas, *The Opulent Eye*, Architectural Press, London, 1976

Cornforth, John, *The Search for a Style: Country Life and Architecture 1897–1935*, André Deutsch, London, 1988.

Du Cane, Ella and Florence, *The Flowers and Gardens of Japan*, Adam and Charles Black, London, 1908.

Edwards, Paul, and Swift, Katherine, *Pergolas, Arbours and Arches*, Barn Elms, London, 2001.

Everett, Nigel, *Wild Gardens: the Lost Demesnes of Bantry Bay*, Hafod Press, Bantry, Co. Cork, 2000.

Fouquier, Marcel, *De L'Art des Jardins du XVe au XX Siècle*, Paris, 1911.

Garden Furniture and Ornament [Catalogue of J. P. White's Pyghtle Works of Bedford], Apollo Books, New York, 1987.

Godfrey, Walter Hindes, *Gardens in the Making*, Batsford, London, 1914.

Grainger, Hilary, *The Architecture of Sir Ernest George and His Partners, c.1860–1922*, University of Leeds, PhD, 1985.

Gray, A. Stuart, *Edwardian Architecture: a Biographical Dictionary*, Duckworth, London, 1985.

Hadfield, Miles, *A History of British Gardening*, Spring Books, London, 1969.

Hazlehurst, Franklin Hamilton, *Jacques Boyceau and the French Formal Garden*, University of Georgia Press, Athens, 1966.

Helmreich, Anne, *The English Garden and National Identity: the Competing Styles of Garden Design, 1870–1914*, Cambridge University Press, Cambridge, 2002.

Hitchmough, Wendy, *Arts and Crafts Gardens*, Pavilion, London, 1997.

Hobhouse, Penelope, *Private Gardens of England*, Weidenfeld & Nicolson, London, 1986.

Holme, Charles, *The Gardens of England*, 3v, The Studio, London, 1907, 1908, & 1911.

Iford Manor and its Garden, *Architectural Review*, v. 33, 1913, 11–14 & 28–30.

Jekyll, Gertrude, *Garden Ornament*, Country Life, London, 1918, & 2nd edition, 1927.

—, and Weaver, Lawrence, *Gardens for Small Country Houses*, Country Life, London, 1912.

Jennings, Anne, *Edwardian Gardens*, English Heritage, London, 2005.

Malins, Edward, and Bowe, Patrick, *Irish Gardens and Demesnes from 1830*, Barrie & Jenkins, London, 1980.

Masson, Georgina, *Italian Villas and Palaces*, Thames & Hudson, London, 1959.

—, *Italian Gardens*, Thames & Hudson, London, 1961.

Maumene, Albert, Le Jardin à L'Antique de Maryland. *La Vie à la Campagne*, 1 January 1911.

Mawson, Thomas H., *The Art and Craft of Garden Making*, Batsford and Newnes, London, 1900.

Moore, Graeme, Renaissance d'Azur, *Country Life*, 7 July, 1988.

Mowl, Timothy, *Historic Gardens of Wiltshire*, Tempus, Stroud, 2004.

—, *Historic Gardens of Dorset*, Tempus, Stroud, 2003.

Musson, Jeremy, *The English Manor House: From the Archives of Country Life*, Aurum Press, London, 1999.

Newall, Peter, *Mauretania: Triumph and Resurrection*, J. & M. Clarkson, Preston, 2006.

Nichols, Rose Standish, *English Pleasure Gardens*, Macmillan, New York, 1902.

—, *Italian Pleasure Gardens*, Williams & Norgate, London, 1929.

—, *Spanish and Portuguese Gardens*, Constable, London, 1929.

Ottewill, David, *The Edwardian Garden*, Yale University Press, New Haven and London, 1989.

Peto, Harold A., *The Boke of Iford*, with an historical introduction by Robin Whalley, Libanus Press, Marlborough, 1993.

Quest-Ritson, Charles, *The English Garden Abroad*, Viking, London, 1992.

Richardson, Tim, *English Gardens in the Twentieth Century*, Aurum Press, London, 2005.

Robinson, William, *The Wild Garden*, John Murray, London, 1870.

Sedding, John Dando, *Garden-Craft Old and New*, Kegan Paul & Co, London, 1891.

Sir Lawrence Alma-Tadema, Catalogue of an exhibition held at the Van Gogh Museum, Amsterdam, 1996–97 and at the Walker Art Gallery, Liverpool, 1997.

Tankard, Judith, *Gardens of the Arts and Crafts Movement*, Abrams, New York, 2004.

Taylor, G. C., *The Modern Garden*, Country Life, London, 1936.

Tilden, Philip, *True Remembrances*, Country Life, London, 1954.

Tipping, H. Avray, *English Gardens*, Country Life, London, 1925.

Triggs, H. Inigo, *The Art of Garden Design in Italy*, London, 1906.

—, *Formal Gardens in England and Scotland*, Batsford, London, 1902.

—, *Garden Craft in Europe*, Batsford, London, 1913.

Villiers-Stuart, C. M., *Spanish Gardens*, Batsford, London, 1929.

Whalley, Robin, Harold Peto: Shadows from Pompeii and the Work of Sir Lawrence Alma-Tadema. *Garden History*, 33 (2), Winter 2005.

—, Harold Peto's Japanese Diary, *Hortus*, 36, Winter 1995, and 37, Spring, 1996.

—, Harold Peto's Spanish Diary 1888, *Hortus* 55, Autumn 2000.

—, The Plantsman of Iford Manor, *Journal of the Wiltshire Gardens Trust*, 31, Spring 1995.

Woodbridge, Kenneth, *Princely Gardens: the Origin and Development of the French Formal Style*, Thames & Hudson, London, 1986.